MIDDAY MEALS

AUTHOR: JENI WRIGHT

CELEBRITY COOK: MICHAEL SMITH

CONTENTS

First published in 1985 by Octopus Books Limited
59 Grosvenor Street, London W1
© 1985 Hennerwood Publications Limited
ISBN 0 86273 191 7
Printed and bound by Jarrold and Sons Ltd at Norwich

NOTE

1. All recipes serve four unless otherwise stated.
2. All spoon measurements are level. Spoon measures can be bought in both imperial and metric sizes to give accurate measurement of small quantities.
3. All eggs are size 2 or 3 unless otherwise stated.
4. All sugar is granulated unless otherwise stated.
5. Preparation times given are an average calculated during recipe testing.
6. Metric and imperial measurements have been calculated separately. Use one set of measurements only as they are not exact equivalents.
7. Cooking times may vary slightly depending on the individual oven. Dishes should be placed in the centre of an oven unless otherwise specified.
8. Always preheat the oven or grill to the specified temperature.
9. (F) indicates at which point a dish can be frozen. (A) indicates up to which point the dish can be prepared in advance. Brief freezing and/or advance preparation details can be found at the end of all recipes in which these symbols have been included.
10. The symbol (M) precedes information on thawing and reheating dishes in a microwave cooker. The information is based on a cooker having a 650 watt output.

DISHES IN ADVANCE

Whether you're planning a simple family lunch, or a more elaborate dish because friends are invited round, you'll appreciate the carefree cooking of the recipes in this section.

As the title suggests, all the dishes can be prepared in advance, either a few hours ahead, the night before, or even up to two days beforehand in some cases. With the main dish for lunch out of the way you are left with plenty of time to do last-minute shopping for fresh salad vegetables, bread and such, or to prepare salads and vegetable accompaniments ready to be freshly put together just before serving. So there is no need to have a harassed morning slaving over a hot stove. You can get organized well in advance with these recipes.

Smoked trout has a subtle flavour when combined with soft cheese, lemon, horseradish and cream. If you prefer a more pronounced smoky flavour, use smoked mackerel instead. It is more widely available, slightly less expensive, and comes conveniently filleted.

SMOKED TROUT CHARLOTTE

Serves 8

vegetable oil, for brushing

175 g (6 oz) thinly sliced smoked salmon

3 tablespoons lemon juice

1 tablespoon powdered gelatine

175-200 g (6-7 oz) smoked trout

450 g (1 lb) full-fat soft cheese

2 tablespoons creamed horseradish

freshly ground black pepper

150 ml (¼ pint) double cream

2 egg whites

To garnish:

lemon slices

Preparation time: *45 minutes, plus overnight chilling*

1 Brush the inside of a 1.25-1.50 litre (2¼-2¾ pint) charlotte tin lightly with oil. Line the base with a circle of grease-proof paper, then oil the paper. Line the tin with the slices of smoked salmon, making sure there are no gaps. Chop any leftover salmon and reserve.

2 Pour the lemon juice into a heat-proof measuring jug and make up to 150 ml (¼ pint) with water. Sprinkle the gelatine over the liquid and leave to stand until spongy. Place the jug in a saucepan of gently simmering water and heat until the gelatine has dissolved. Leave to cool slightly.

3 Meanwhile, skin and bone the trout, then flake the flesh into a bowl. Add the cheese and horseradish, with pepper to taste, and beat well.

4 Stir the gelatine liquid into the fish mixture until evenly incorporated. Whip the cream until it just holds its shape, then beat the egg whites in a separate bowl until stiff. Fold the cream into the fish mixture until evenly incorporated, then add the egg whites.

5 Spoon the mixture into the lined tin. (If there is any leftover chopped salmon, put this in the middle of the mousse after spooning half the mousse into the tin.) Cover the tin with lightly oiled foil and chill in the refrigerator overnight. **A**

6 When ready to serve, run a palette knife between the smoked salmon and the tin. Turn out on to a serving plate and garnish with lemon. Serve chilled for a special lunch party, with whole-wheat or granary bread or toast.

A Chill for up to 3 days.

SPINACH AND RICOTTA ROLL

Serves 4-6

450 g (1 lb) frozen spinach

225 g (8 oz) ricotta cheese

1 egg, beaten

¼ teaspoon freshly grated nutmeg

salt

freshly ground black pepper

1 × 375 g (13 oz) packet frozen puff pastry, thawed

25 g (1 oz) butter, melted

50 g (2 oz) Parmesan cheese, freshly grated

Preparation time: *about 20 minutes, plus cooling*
Cooking time: *about 1½ hours*
Oven: *200°C, 400°F, Gas Mark 6*

1 Put the frozen spinach in a heavy-based saucepan and heat very gently for 10-15 minutes until thawed. Increase the heat and drive off any excess liquid (the spinach should be as dry as possible), then turn into a bowl and leave until cold.

2 Add the ricotta cheese, egg and nutmeg to the spinach, with salt and pepper to taste. Beat well to mix.

3 Roll out the pastry on a floured surface to a 35 × 30 cm (14 × 12 inch) rectangle. Spread the spinach mixture over the pastry, leaving a narrow margin around the edges.

4 Roll up the pastry from one long side like a Swiss roll. Place, seam side down, on a sheet of lightly buttered non-stick silicone paper, then wrap in the paper, folding in the ends to enclose the roll completely. Overwrap in the same way with a sheet of foil. **F**

5 Place the roll in a fish kettle, large oval casserole or deep roasting tin. Cover with boiling water, then cover and simmer for 1 hour. Turn once during cooking. Remove from the water and leave to cool. **A**

6 Unwrap the cold roulade and slice thickly. Arrange the slices in an oven-proof gratin dish and pour over the melted butter. Sprinkle with the Parmesan cheese and cook in a preheated oven for 15 minutes. Serve hot.

A Keep in a cold place overnight.

F Freeze in the wrapping for up to 3 months. Cook from frozen, allowing an extra 15 minutes cooking time.

Smoked Trout Charlotte; Spinach and Ricotta Roll

MOZZARELLA MEAT LOAF

Serves 4-6

500 g (1¼ lb) lean minced beef

1 small onion, peeled and finely chopped

50 g (2 oz) fresh wholewheat breadcrumbs

2 tablespoons tomato purée

2 tablespoons chopped fresh parsley

1 teaspoon dried basil

1 teaspoon dried oregano

salt

freshly ground black pepper

1 egg, beaten

2 × 120 g (4½ oz) packets Mozzarella cheese, sliced

Tomato Sauce:

2 tablespoons olive or vegetable oil

1 small onion, peeled and finely chopped

1 garlic clove, peeled and crushed

1 × 400 g (14 oz) can tomatoes

150 ml (¼ pint) water

1 tablespoon tomato purée

1 tablespoon red wine vinegar

½ teaspoon dried mixed herbs

½ teaspoon dried oregano

pinch of sugar

Preparation time: *20 minutes, plus standing*
Cooking time: *about 1¾ hours*
Oven: *200°C, 400°F, Gas Mark 6*

1 To make the tomato sauce, heat the oil in a pan, add the onion and garlic and fry gently until soft. Add the remaining ingredients and salt and pepper, bring to the boil, stirring to break up the tomatoes. Cover and simmer for 30 minutes, stirring occasionally. **A F M**

2 Meanwhile, put the minced beef in a bowl with the onion, breadcrumbs, tomato purée, herbs and salt and pepper to taste. Mix with your hands until well combined, then bind with the beaten egg.

3 Brush the inside of a 1 kg (2 lb) loaf tin lightly with oil and line the base with greaseproof paper. Brush the paper with oil. Press a layer of the beef mixture in the bottom and up the sides of the tin. Arrange half of the Mozzarella slices in a layer on top of the beef, then cover with about half of the remaining beef. Repeat these 2 layers with the remaining cheese and beef, pressing down well. Cover with foil. **A**

4 Cook the meat loaf, covered, in a preheated oven for 1 hour. Remove from the oven, carefully pour off the excess juices and then leave to stand for 10 minutes. During this time, reheat the sauce until bubbling, stirring frequently. Taste and adjust the seasoning.

5 To serve, turn the meat loaf out on to a warmed serving plate and pour over a little of the sauce. Hand the remaining sauce separately in a sauceboat or jug.

6 Serve with French bread, a bottle of red wine, and a green salad.

A Leave the tomato sauce to go cold, then refrigerate for up to 2 days. The meat loaf can be chilled in the refrigerator for 2 hours before cooking.

F Freeze the tomato sauce in a rigid container for up to 3 months. Heat from frozen.

M To thaw the tomato sauce, turn out into suitable container. Cook on defrost power for 10 minutes breaking up with a fork when possible. Cook on maximum (full) power for 6 minutes, stir before serving.

SESAME FISHCAKES

Makes 12-14

750 g (1½ lb) old potatoes, peeled

salt

450 g (1 lb) smoked haddock fillets

300 ml (½ pint) milk

1 bay leaf

2 slices of onion

6 black peppercorns

25 g (1 oz) unsalted butter

2 tablespoons chopped fresh parsley

freshly ground black pepper

2 tablespoons plain flour

100 g (4 oz) stale white or dried breadcrumbs

4 tablespoons sesame seeds

1 egg

vegetable oil, for shallow frying

To garnish:

sprigs of parsley

Preparation time: *30 minutes, plus chilling*
Cooking time: *about 45 minutes (about 55 minutes if frying in 2 batches)*

1 Cook the potatoes in boiling salted water for 20-25 minutes until tender.

2 Meanwhile, put the smoked haddock in a separate pan. Add the milk, bay leaf, onion slices and peppercorns,

cover and simmer for 10 minutes or until the fish flakes easily when tested with a fork. Remove the fish from the milk and flake the flesh, discarding the skin and bones.

3 Drain the potatoes and mash them with the butter and 2 tablespoons of the milk in which the fish was cooked. Add the flaked fish and parsley. Sprinkle with a little salt and plenty of black pepper. Allow to cool slightly if still hot, then shape into 12-14 fishcakes.

4 Spread the flour out on a flat plate. Combine the breadcrumbs and sesame seeds together on another plate. Beat the egg in a shallow dish.

5 Coat the fishcakes first in the flour, then dip in the beaten egg and coat in the breadcrumb and sesame mixture. Chill in the refrigerator for at least 1 hour. **A** **F**

6 To serve, heat the oil in a frying pan, add the fishcakes and fry over a moderate heat for 3-5 minutes on each side until golden brown and crisp. (If your pan is not large enough, you may have to fry them in 2 batches.) Drain on paper towels before serving. Garnish with sprigs of parsley.

7 Serve for a family lunch with French fries and a seasonal green vegetable such as creamed fresh spinach, or a mixed salad.

A The fishcakes can be chilled overnight.

F Open freeze, then cover and freeze the fishcakes for up to 1 month. Cook from frozen, allowing slightly more cooking time.

Mozzarella Meatloaf; Sesame Fishcakes

CHICKEN CASSEROLE WITH MANGO

500 g (1¼ lb) boneless chicken
breasts, skinned and cut into
bite-size pieces

2 tablespoons soy sauce

2 tablespoons honey

2.5 cm (1 inch) fresh root ginger,
peeled and crushed

2 garlic cloves, peeled and crushed

½ teaspoon ground mixed spice

freshly ground black pepper

15 g (½ oz) butter

1 tablespoon vegetable oil

2 teaspoons cornflour

150 ml (¼ pint) water

150 ml (¼ pint) orange juice

salt

½ ripe mango, skinned

*Preparation time: 15 minutes,
plus marinating
Cooking time: 40 minutes*

1 Place the chicken pieces in a bowl. Add the soy sauce, honey, ginger, garlic, mixed spice and pepper to taste. Stir well to mix, then cover and marinate for at least 2 hours in the refrigerator. **A**

2 Melt the butter with the oil in a flameproof casserole. Remove the chicken from the marinade with a slotted spoon and add to the casserole. Fry over moderate heat, stirring until lightly coloured on all sides.

3 Pour the marinade into the casserole. Blend the cornflour with a little of the water, then add the orange juice and water to the casserole. Cut half the mango into diamond shapes and reserve. Roughly chop the remainder and add to the casserole. Cover and simmer for 30 minutes or until the chicken is tender. **F** **M**

4 Arrange the mango diamonds on top. Cover and heat through for 5 minutes. Serve with rice or noodles.

A The chicken can be marinated for up to 24 hours before cooking.

F Cool, then turn into a rigid container and freeze for up to 3 months. Thaw for 4-6 hours, reheat until bubbling.

M To thaw, cook on defrost power covered loosely for 20-25 minutes, break up with a fork. Stand for 15 minutes. Cook on maximum (full) power for 15-20 minutes, covered.

CREAMY CAMEMBERT QUICHE

Serves 4-6

50 g (2 oz) butter

1 tablespoon olive oil

2 medium onions, peeled and
thinly sliced

275 g (10 oz) frozen shortcrust
pastry, thawed

1-2 garlic cloves, peeled and crushed

225 g (8 oz) soft, ripe Camembert
cheese

3 eggs, beaten

8 tablespoons double cream

salt

freshly ground black pepper

*Preparation time: 20 minutes
Cooking time: about 1¼ hours,
plus standing
Oven: 200°C, 400°F, Gas Mark 6;
then 180°C, 350°F, Gas Mark 4*

1 To prepare the filling, melt the butter with the oil in a heavy-based saucepan. Add the onions and fry very gently, stirring frequently, for 20 minutes until very soft and light golden.

2 Meanwhile, roll out the pastry on a floured surface and use to line a 23 cm (9

Baking 'blind' may seem time-consuming if you are in a hurry when making pastry dishes, but it should not be omitted in recipes such as this one which have relatively runny fillings or the finished pastry base will be uncooked and soggy. Baking 'blind' with a mock filling of greaseproof paper or foil and beans gives a crisp, set pastry before the filling is added, thus preventing moisture seeping through and resulting in a soggy base.

*Chicken Casserole
with Mango; Suffolk
Pub Steak Pies*

inch) loose-bottomed metal flan tin. Prick the base with a fork, then line with foil and baking beans. Bake 'blind' in a preheated oven for 15 minutes, then remove the foil and beans and bake for a further 7 minutes until the pastry is set. **A** Reduce the oven temperature.

3 Add the garlic to the onions and fry for a few minutes until softened. Transfer to a bowl.

4 Cut the rind off the Camembert, then cut the cheese into small pieces and add to the onions. Mash with a fork to break up the cheese. Add the eggs and cream with salt and pepper to taste and beat well to mix. **A**

5 Pour the fillings into the pastry case. Bake on a hot baking sheet in a preheated oven for 30-35 minutes until the filling is just set. Leave to stand for 15 minutes before slicing.

6 Serve with a tomato salad.

A The pastry case can be prepared and baked blind up to 2 days in advance and stored in an airtight tin. The filling can be chilled overnight.

SUFFOLK PUB STEAK PIES

3 tablespoons vegetable oil
1 kg (2 lb) chuck steak, trimmed of fat and cut into thin strips
1 onion, peeled and chopped
2 tablespoons mushroom ketchup
1 teaspoon dried mixed herbs
1 × 275 ml (9 fl oz) can sweet stout
300 ml (½ pint) beef stock or water
salt
freshly ground black pepper
15 g (½ oz) butter
225 g (8 oz) button mushrooms, sliced
1 × 375 g (13 oz) packet frozen puff pastry, thawed
beaten egg, to glaze

Preparation time: 30-40 minutes, plus cooling
Cooking time: 2½-2¾ hours
Oven: 160°C, 325°F, Gas Mark 3; then 200°C, 400°F, Gas Mark 6

1 Heat the oil in a flameproof casserole, add the beef and fry over brisk heat until browned on all sides. Remove with a slotted spoon and set aside.

2 Lower the heat, add the onion to the casserole and fry gently until soft. Stir in the mushroom ketchup and the herbs, then the meat, sweet stout and stock or water. Bring slowly to the boil, add salt and pepper. Cover and cook in a preheated oven (at the lower temperature) for 2 hours until the beef is tender.

3 Melt the butter in a frying pan, add the mushrooms and fry over moderate heat until the juices run, shaking the pan frequently. Stir the mushrooms and juices into the casserole. Cool. **A**

4 Divide the cold beef filling equally between 4 individual pie dishes, then cover with pastry lids (see below). **F** Brush with beaten egg to glaze.

5 Bake the pies on a hot baking sheet in a preheated oven (at the higher temperature) for 30 minutes until the filling is bubbling and the pastry is golden brown. Cover the pies with foil or greaseproof if they show signs of overbrowning. Before serving, enlarge the holes to reveal the filling.

6 Serve hot, straight from the pie dishes, with glasses of beer.

A The beef filling can be cooked up to 2 days in advance and chilled.

F Open freeze the unbaked pies, then wrap individually in polythene bags. Unwrap and thaw for 4-6 hours, glaze the pastry, then bake as in the recipe.

The mushroom ketchup in the Suffolk pub steak pies is available in bottles from delicatessens and some large supermarkets. Made from mushrooms, vinegar and soy, it is very strong in flavour, and gives a wonderfully rich mushroomy 'kick' to all kinds of casseroles, sauces and soups. It is a very useful ingredient to have in your storecupboard as it keeps indefinitely.

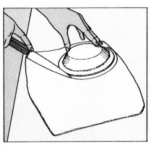

1 *Roll out the pastry on a lightly floured surface and cut out 4 shapes slightly larger than the pie dishes.*

2 *Add the pie filling. Cut out 4 strips the width and length of the dish rims. Brush the rims with water; press the strips firmly on top.*

3 *Brush the pastry strips with water, then put the lids on, pressing the edges to seal.*

4 *Knock up the edges, then flute, or scallop, with your forefinger and thumb, or a knife. Make a hole and decorate with trimmings.*

SAME DAY SPECIALS

The quick and easy recipes in this section are intended both to liven up your tastebuds at lunchtime, and to prove that delicious dishes *can* be prepared and cooked in next to no time.

Lunch is often a busy time of the day and the temptation is to grab a quick bite such as a sandwich, biscuits and cheese, or a bowl of fruit and yogurt. These are all very well once in a while but they do not provide a substantial meal and can become boring if repeated too often. Whatever your lifestyle, try to find time to sit down and relax over lunch. It will give you far more energy for the rest of the day, so it's time well spent.

The preparation of lunch needn't be as precise and demanding as the main evening meal. Save time by mixing convenience foods with fresh ingredients, no-one will be able to tell!

Clockwise, from left: Cottage Cheese Cocottes; Bacon and Avocado Grills

Take care when scrambling the eggs for Scotch woodcock – keep the heat low and remove the scrambled eggs from the pan immediately they start to set. If the eggs are left in the pan, the heat of the pan will continue to cook the eggs and they will become rubbery.

SCOTCH WOODCOCK

2 × 50 g (2 oz) cans anchovy fillets, drained and soaked in milk for 20 minutes
150 g (5 oz) unsalted butter
2 teaspoons chopped fresh parsley
2 teaspoons lemon juice
freshly ground black pepper
5 eggs
150 ml (¼ pint) single cream
4 slices of wholewheat or granary bread
salt

Preparation time: 10 minutes, plus soaking
Cooking time: 10 minutes

1 Drain the anchovies and pat dry with paper towels. Chop 6 of the anchovies finely, then beat into 100 g (4 oz) of the butter with the parsley, lemon juice and pepper to taste. **A**
2 Beat the eggs lightly with the cream. Set aside. Toast the bread on both sides, then spread with the anchovy butter. Keep hot.
3 Melt the remaining butter in a heavy-based saucepan. Pour in the egg and cream mixture and stir over low heat until the eggs are just set. Add a little salt and plenty of pepper.
4 Spoon the scrambled eggs on top of the toast then garnish with anchovies.
5 Serve at once with grilled tomatoes.
A The anchovy butter can be made 2 days in advance and chilled. Soften at room temperature before using.

COTTAGE CHEESE COCOTTES

Serves 2
25 g (1 oz) butter
1 small onion, peeled and finely chopped
½ teaspoon paprika
1 × 225 g (8 oz) carton cottage cheese
50 g (2 oz) boiled ham, diced
50 g (2 oz) button mushrooms, sliced
2 strips of canned pimento, diced (optional)
2 eggs, beaten
salt
freshly ground black pepper

Preparation time: 15 minutes
Cooking time: 30-40 minutes
Oven: 200°C, 400°F, Gas Mark 6

1 Melt the butter in a small saucepan, add the onion and fry gently for 5 minutes until soft. Add the paprika and fry for 1 minute, stirring constantly.
2 Transfer the onion to a bowl, then add the remaining ingredients, with salt and pepper to taste. Beat well to mix.
3 Turn the mixture into two 300 ml (½ pint) ovenproof dishes. Bake in a preheated oven for 25-30 minutes until set and golden brown.
4 Serve at once with fingers of toast.

BACON AND AVOCADO GRILLS

Serves 2
50 g (2 oz) butter
1 medium dessert apple, cored and sliced
4 tablespoons lemon juice
3 rashers of middle cut bacon, rinded and cut into strips
2 tablespoons flour
300 ml (½ pint) milk
100 g (4 oz) Caerphilly cheese, grated
salt
freshly ground black pepper
1 ripe avocado
about 4 tablespoons dried wholewheat breadcrumbs

Preparation time: 20 minutes
Cooking time: 25-30 minutes
Oven: 200°C, 400°F, Gas Mark 6

1 Melt the butter in a heavy-based saucepan, add the apple and fry gently for 2-3 minutes until lightly coloured. Remove with a slotted spoon to a plate and sprinkle with half the lemon juice.
2 Add the bacon to the pan, increase the heat to moderate and fry until quite crisp. Sprinkle in the flour and cook, stirring, for 1-2 minutes. Remove from the heat and gradually beat in the milk.
3 Return to the heat and simmer, stirring, until thick and smooth. Stir in two-thirds of the cheese, add salt and pepper, then simmer until melted.
4 Quickly peel, halve and stone the avocado. Cut into slices and sprinkle with remaining lemon juice. Arrange the avocado and apple slices in 2 gratin dishes, then pour over the sauce.
5 Mix the breadcrumbs with the remaining cheese and sprinkle over the top. Bake on a hot baking sheet in a preheated oven for 10-15 minutes.
6 Serve with hot buttered toast.

Blocks of creamed coconut are available in packets at supermarkets and delicatessens. Creamed coconut is very rich and smooth, and makes wonderfully creamy sauces; it is very concentrated and therefore a little goes a long way.

COCONUT PRAWNS

2 tablespoons vegetable oil

1 tablespoon sesame oil

1 small onion, peeled and finely chopped

1 garlic clove, peeled and crushed

2.5 cm (1 inch) piece of fresh root ginger, peeled and crushed

2 teaspoons ground turmeric

225 g (8 oz) frozen prawns

finely grated rind of 1 lime

2 tablespoons lime juice

50 g (2 oz) creamed coconut

150 ml (¼ pint) water

salt

freshly ground black pepper

225 g (8 oz) frozen white fish steaks (e.g. haddock or cod), cut into bite sized cubes

To garnish:

a few lime slices

Preparation time: 10 minutes
Cooking time: 25 minutes

1 Heat the oils in a heavy-based frying pan. Add the onion, garlic, ginger and turmeric and fry gently for 5 minutes, stirring constantly, until soft.

2 Add the prawns and stir-fry until defrosted and coated in the onion mixture, then add the grated lime rind and juice and stir well to mix.

3 Grate or crumble two-thirds of the coconut into the pan, then pour in the water and bring to the boil, stirring. Add salt and pepper to taste. **A**

4 Add the frozen cubes of fish and cook for 5 minutes or until thawed and tender (do not overcook or the fish will disintegrate). Taste and adjust the seasoning, then turn into a warmed serving dish. Grate the remaining coconut over the top and garnish with lime.

5 Serve with rice, a green salad and yogurt, cucumber and fresh mint raita.

A The dish can be made up to this stage the night before. Leave to cool, then chill. On the day reheat until bubbling before continuing.

In coastal areas of Italy, fresh clams are used instead of the bottled ones suggested in this recipe for spaghetti alle vongole. Fresh clams are bought in the early morning at the fish market and this dish is often made for lunch, with a garnish of a few clams in their shells. Fresh clams are difficult to obtain here, but bottled ones make a good substitute. Some delicatessens sell bottles of clams in their shells which could be used to make the dish look more authentic.

SPAGHETTI ALLE VONGOLE

Serves 2

2 tablespoons olive oil

1 garlic clove, peeled and crushed

1 × 225 g (8 oz) can tomatoes

1 × 120 g (4½ oz) jar natural clams

½ teaspoon dried basil

½ teaspoon dried oregano

salt

freshly ground black pepper

175 g (6 oz) spaghetti

15 g (½ oz) butter

Preparation time: *5 minutes*
Cooking time: *about 20 minutes*

1 Heat the oil in a heavy-based saucepan, add the garlic and fry gently until soft. Purée the tomatoes and their juice in a blender or food processor. Add to the pan and bring to the boil.

2 Drain the clams and measure 150 ml (¼ pint) of the juice. Add the juice to the pan with the herbs and salt and pepper to taste. Simmer for 10 minutes.

3 Meanwhile, cook the spaghetti in a separate large pan of boiling salted water for 12 minutes or according to packet instructions.

4 Stir the clams into the tomato sauce and simmer for a further 5 minutes. Taste and adjust the seasoning of the sauce. **A** **F** **M**

5 Drain the spaghetti thoroughly, then return to the pan with the butter and toss vigorously until the butter has melted and coated the spaghetti. Put the spaghetti in a warmed serving dish, pour the sauce over the top and serve immediately.

6 Serve with a green salad tossed in an olive oil and lemon juice dressing.

A The clam sauce can be made the night before. Leave to cool then keep in the refrigerator. On the day reheat until bubbling and cook the spaghetti.

F Freeze the clam sauce in a rigid container for up to one month. Reheat from frozen, adding a little water to prevent the sauce sticking.

M To thaw, turn the sauce into a suitable container. Cook on defrost power for 6-10 minutes breaking up with a fork when possible. Cook on maximum (full) power for 4-6 minutes, stir before serving.

Clockwise, from left: Coconut Prawns with green salad and raita; Spaghetti alle vongole

CYPRUS SOUFFLÉ

Serves 2

40 g (1½ oz) butter

25 g (1 oz) flour

150 ml (¼ pint) milk

100 g (4 oz) Feta cheese, crumbled

freshly ground black pepper

3 eggs, separated

1 medium firm tomato, skinned and finely diced

25 g (1 oz) black olives, stoned and finely chopped

2 tablespoons chopped fresh coriander or fresh parsley

Preparation time: *20 minutes*
Cooking time: *35-40 minutes*
Oven: *200°C, 400°F, Gas Mark 6*

1 Melt the butter in a heavy-based saucepan, sprinkle in the flour and cook, stirring, for 1-2 minutes. Remove from the heat and beat in the milk a little at a time.

2 Return to the heat and simmer, stirring, until very thick and smooth. Stir in the cheese and pepper to taste, then simmer for a further few minutes until the cheese has melted. Remove from the heat, stir in the egg yolks and leave to cool. **A**

3 Meanwhile, whisk the egg whites until stiff.

4 When the cheese sauce is cold, stir in the tomato and olives, together with the coriander or parsley.

5 Fold in the egg whites until evenly incorporated, then turn the mixture immediately into a well-buttered 750 ml (1¼ pint) soufflé dish or pudding basin. Bake immediately on a hot baking sheet in a preheated oven for 25-30 minutes until risen and golden brown. Serve at once.

6 Serve for an unusual light lunch, with fingers of hot wholemeal pitta bread and glasses of chilled white Retsina wine.

A The cheese sauce can be made several hours in advance and kept covered.

Feta cheese has good melting qualities and is therefore excellent for cooking in soufflés. Look for it pre-packaged in large supermarkets; specialist cheese shops and Greek and Cypriot stores sell it loose by the kg (lb). When sold loose the cheese may be particularly salty so soak it for 1 hour in cold water, then pat dry before using.

CHICKEN CRUMBLE

4 portions cooked chicken
50 g (2 oz) butter
175 g (6 oz) button mushrooms,
wiped and sliced
2 tablespoons flour
300 ml (½ pint) milk
1 teaspoon French mustard
100 g (4 oz) Gruyère cheese, grated
freshly ground black pepper
2 × 25 g (1 oz) packets plain salted
crisps, finely crushed
25 g (1 oz) finely chopped
fresh parsley

Preparation time: 20 minutes
Cooking time: 20 minutes

1 Remove the chicken flesh from the bones, discarding all skin, and cut into bite-sized cubes. Set aside.
2 Melt the butter in a heavy-based saucepan, add the mushrooms and fry gently for 5 minutes. Sprinkle in the flour and cook, stirring, for 1-2 minutes. Remove from the heat and beat in the milk a little at a time.
3 Return to the heat and simmer, stirring, until thick and smooth. Stir in the mustard and cheese, add pepper to taste, then simmer for a further few minutes until the cheese has melted.
4 Remove the pan from the heat and fold in the cubed chicken. **A** **F** **M** Transfer to a flameproof serving dish. Mix together the crushed crisps and parsley and sprinkle over the top. Place under a preheated moderate grill for a few minutes to brown the topping.
5 Serve with a seasonal green vegetable such as courgettes, French beans or mange-touts, tossed in butter with finely chopped fresh herbs and plenty of freshly ground black pepper.
A The chicken in cheese sauce can be made up to 24 hours in advance. Cool then keep in the refrigerator. Reheat until bubbling before continuing with the recipe.
F Allow to cool then freeze the chicken in cheese sauce in a rigid container for up to 1 month. Add the topping, then cook from frozen in a preheated moderately hot oven 200°C, 400°F, Gas Mark 6 for 45 minutes.
M To thaw, cook loosely covered on defrost power for 15-20 minutes. Break up with a fork when possible. Complete as above.

FRITTATA

6 eggs
300 ml (½ pint) milk
100 g (4 oz) Parma ham, cut into
thin strips
50 g (2 oz) pine nuts, roughly chopped
5 tablespoons dried breadcrumbs
4 tablespoons freshly grated
Parmesan cheese
2 tablespoons chopped fresh parsley
pinch of freshly grated nutmeg
salt
freshly ground black pepper
2 tablespoons olive oil
1 small onion, peeled and
finely chopped

Preparation time: 20 minutes
Cooking time: 30-35 minutes

1 Put the eggs in a bowl with the milk, ham, pine nuts, breadcrumbs, cheese, parsley and nutmeg. Add the salt and pepper to taste and beat well to mix. **A**
2 Heat half the oil in a large, heavy-based frying pan, add half of the chopped onion and fry gently for 5 minutes until soft. Pour in the egg mixture, increase the heat and allow to bubble for 1 minute.
3 Lower the heat, cover and cook very gently for 15 minutes until the underside of the frittata is browned and the centre is no longer runny.
4 Place a large plate on top of the frying pan and turn the frittata out on to it. Set aside. Wipe the inside of the pan clean with a paper towel. Heat the remaining oil in the pan, add the remaining onion and fry gently until soft.
5 Return the frittata to the pan browned side uppermost. Cover and cook gently for 5 minutes. Slide out on to a warmed serving plate and cut into wedges. **A**
6 Serve hot or cold with a tomato, fennel and fresh basil salad.
A The ingredients for the frittata can be mixed together up to 4 hours in advance. If to be served cold the frittata can be cooked up to 24 hours in advance, and kept, covered, in the refrigerator.

A frittata is an Italian omelette, not to be confused with the French kind of omelette which is cooked for a very short time and served folded in two or three. Frittata is similar to the Spanish tortilla – cooked on both sides and served flat. In Italy frittata is often cooked for picnics because it is delicious served cold, cut into wedges.

Peach and Hazelnut Salad; Frittata

PEACH AND HAZELNUT SALAD

6 tablespoons vegetable oil

2 tablespoons lemon juice

salt

freshly ground black pepper

225 g (8 oz) Gorgonzola cheese, rind removed

15 g (½ oz) unsalted butter, softened

2 teaspoons single cream or top of the milk

3 medium ripe peaches, skinned, halved and stones removed

1 head radicchio washed and shredded

1 bunch watercress, trimmed and washed

100 g (4 oz) shelled hazelnuts, roughly chopped

Preparation time: 30 minutes

1 In a large bowl, whisk the oil and lemon juice with salt and pepper to taste. Chop half of the Gorgonzola and add to the dressing. Set aside.

2 Put the remaining Gorgonzola in a separate bowl and mash with a fork, adding the butter, cream and pepper.

3 Stuff the cavities of the peaches with the creamed Gorgonzola mixture, then cut each peach half in two.

4 Add the radicchio, watercress and nuts to the bowl and toss well to coat in the dressing. Divide the salad equally between 4 individual plates and top each one with 3 peach quarters.

5 Serve immediately with granary bread and butter.

Variation:

In wintertime use pears instead of peaches. Peel and core the pears and brush the flesh with lemon juice.

Italian radicchio is a pretty red-leaved salad ingredient, a member of the chicory family. It is becoming increasingly widely available in the summer months at good supermarkets and specialist greengrocers. If you find it difficult to obtain, use 175-225 g (6-8 oz) shredded red cabbage instead.

NEXT DAY LUNCHES

With a little imagination, and the addition of a few extra ingredients, cooked meats and vegetables can be turned into dishes which are delicious in their own right – and the recipes in this section illustrate just that.

Whoever would think that there is actually a way to use a leftover salad which has sat soggily in vinaigrette dressing overnight? Combined with an onion and potato, and peas from the freezer, it's amazing how good the soupe à la française, based on leftover salad, tastes. One of the secrets of cooking with leftovers is to introduce some fresh ingredients. This is not only important for flavour and colour but fresh ingredients are always more nutritious than anything that has been reheated. This is especially important to bear in mind if you are cooking for young children at lunchtime and lunch is their main meal of the day.

The beansprouts sold in supermarkets, greengrocers and Chinese shops are the sprouting seeds of the mung bean, although other whole seeds are also sprouted such as alfalfa, aduki and soya. All these sprouted seeds and beans are extremely nutritious, especially if eaten raw, so they are a good ingredient to include in everyday cooking – especially if less nutritious leftovers are being used. Beansprouts are rich in protein and amino acids, they also have a high vitamin C content and are a good source of the B vitamins, especially B_1.

CHINESE PORK

5 tablespoons vegetable oil

2 celery sticks, thinly sliced

1 onion, peeled and thinly sliced

1 teaspoon ground ginger

175 g (6 oz) beansprouts

½ cucumber, cut into thin strips

175-225 g (6-8 oz) leftover roast pork, cut into thin strips

4 tablespoons soy sauce

2 tablespoons soft brown sugar

1 tablespoon tomato purée

1 teaspoon French mustard

salt

freshly ground black pepper

300 ml (½ pint) chicken stock

Preparation time: 10-15 minutes
Cooking time: 25 minutes

1 Heat 3 tablespoons of the oil in a wok or large frying pan. Add the celery and onion and stir-fry over a moderate heat for 5 minutes until soft and lightly coloured. Stir in the ginger and fry for 1-2 minutes, stirring all the time.
2 Add the beansprouts and cucumber and stir-fry until heated through. Remove from the pan with a slotted spoon and set aside on a plate.
3 Heat the remaining oil in the pan, add the pork and stir-fry until browned on all sides. Add the soy sauce, sugar, tomato purée, mustard and salt and pepper to taste. Stir well, then pour in the stock and bring to the boil. Simmer, stirring, for a few minutes, then return the vegetables to the pan and stir-fry.
4 Serve at once on a bed of Chinese egg noodles, with extra soy sauce.

SOUPE À LA FRANÇAISE

75 g (3 oz) butter

1 onion, peeled and chopped

275 g (10 oz) potato, peeled and diced

900 ml (1½ pints) vegetable stock or water

225 g (8 oz) frozen peas

leftover dressed green salad (quantity as available)

salt

freshly ground black pepper

1 tablespoon chopped fresh mint or 1 teaspoon dried mint

Preparation time: 15 minutes
Cooking time: 35 minutes

1 Melt the butter in a large, heavy-based saucepan, add the onion and potato and fry very gently for 10 minutes until softened. Pour in the stock or water and bring to the boil, add the peas and cover and simmer for 10 minutes.
2 Drain as much as possible of the dressing from the leftover salad. Add the salad to the pan and continue simmering for a further 10 minutes.
3 Purée the soup in a blender or food processor. Return the soup to the rinsed-out pan. Reheat and thin down with stock or water if necessary. Add salt and pepper to taste, then pour into warmed soup bowls. Sprinkle with mint and serve with herb bread (see right).

MINESTRONE LUNCH BOWL

2 tablespoons olive or vegetable oil

25 g (1 oz) butter

1 small onion, peeled and finely chopped

4 small potatoes, peeled and diced

2 carrots, peeled and thinly sliced

2 celery sticks, thinly sliced

2 tomatoes, skinned and chopped

1 leek, trimmed and thinly sliced

2 teaspoons tomato purée

1.2 litres (2 pints) chicken stock

2 teaspoons dried mixed herbs

salt

freshly ground black pepper

about 175 g (6 oz) leftover boneless cooked chicken, skinned and cubed

100 g (4 oz) frozen peas

about 3 tablespoons freshly grated Parmesan cheese

Preparation time: 20 minutes
Cooking time: 50 minutes

1 Heat the oil and butter in a large heavy-based saucepan. Add the onion and fry gently until soft. Add the remaining vegetables and fry for about 10 minutes, stirring until softened.
2 Add the tomato purée, stock, herbs and salt and pepper. Bring to the boil, half cover and simmer for 20 minutes or until the vegetables are tender.
3 Add the chicken and peas and simmer for a further 10 minutes. **F** Pour into warmed soup bowls.
4 Sprinkle with Parmesan cheese.
F Cool, then freeze in a rigid container for up to 3 months. Reheat from frozen, adding a little water to prevent sticking.

To make herb bread: cut 1 long French stick diagonally into slices about 5 cm (2 inches) thick. Spread the cut surfaces with 225 g (8 oz) softened butter mixed with 4 tablespoons chopped mixed fresh herbs (such as parsley, chives, chervil, basil and marjoram) and freshly ground black pepper to taste. You can also add 1-2 crushed garlic cloves. Wrap the loaf in foil and bake in a preheated oven 180°C, 350°F, Gas Mark 4 for 15 minutes.

The Italian word minestrone is from minestra meaning soup. Minestre in Italy are usually substantial soups with lots of interesting ingredients and minestrone is no exception. There are no hard-and-fast rules about what to add. Italian cooks simply use whatever ingredients they have to hand – such as leftovers of meat, vegetables and pasta.

Clockwise from top: Soupe à la française; Minestrone Lunch Bowl with grated Parmesan cheese; Chinese Pork

Traditional bubble and squeak is made with leftover potatoes (half the quantity should be potato), cabbage and Brussels sprouts, although you can use other vegetables – carrots, for example, give a good colour. Make sure the vegetables are as dry as possible, or the mixture will not fry successfully. If necessary, dry fry the vegetables first in a heavy-based saucepan to drive off excess moisture.

BUBBLE AND SQUEAK WITH CHEESE

Makes 8

about 750 g (1½ lb) cold leftover cooked vegetables (see left)

100 g (4 oz) full-fat soft cheese

1 small onion, peeled and finely chopped

dash of Worcestershire sauce, to taste

1 small egg, beaten

salt

freshly ground black pepper

5-6 tablespoons plain flour

vegetable oil or dripping, for shallow frying

Preparation time: *15 minutes, plus chilling*
Cooking time: *10 minutes (20 minutes if frying in batches)*

1 Mash the vegetables well in a bowl, then add the cheese, onion and Worcestershire sauce and mix thoroughly together. Bind with the beaten egg and add salt and pepper to taste.

2 Divide the mixture roughly into 8 and shape each portion into a triangle. Coat each triangle in the flour. Chill in the refrigerator for at least 30 minutes. **A** **F**

3 Heat the oil or dripping in a heavy-based frying pan until very hot. Add the triangles and fry for about 5 minutes on each side until golden brown and crisp. (You may have to fry in batches or in 2 pans.) Drain on paper towels and serve immediately.

4 Bubble and squeak is traditionally served with cold meat (usually roast beef), and a beetroot and spring onion salad would make a colourful accompaniment. For an extra nutritional lunch, serve the bubble and squeak topped with an egg.

A The vegetable cakes can be stored in the refrigerator for up to 24 hours before frying.

F Open freeze until solid, then pack in a rigid container, separating each cake with film and freeze for up to 3 months. Fry from frozen, allowing extra cooking time.

Bubble and Squeak with Cheese; Exotic Mixed Marinade

EXOTIC MIXED MARINADE

*1 fresh green chilli, with the
seeds discarded (see method)*

*100 g (4 oz) firm white cabbage,
finely shredded*

*¼ large green pepper or ½ small
green pepper, finely shredded*

*¼ cucumber, cut into thin
matchstick strips*

*2.5 cm (1 inch) fresh root ginger,
peeled and finely sliced*

1 large carrot, peeled and grated

*225-275 g (8-10 oz) leftover roast meat
(pork, lamb, chicken), sliced into
thin, even-sized strips*

2 teaspoons sesame seeds

4 tablespoons clear honey

4 tablespoons dry sherry

2 tablespoons soy sauce

150 ml (¼ pint) water

salt

freshly ground black pepper

Preparation time: *30 minutes,
plus marinating*
Cooking time: *5 minutes*

1 The seeds are the hottest part of chillies. Remove them before using the chilli or include a few as you prefer, according to taste.

2 Mix the vegetables together in a shallow serving dish. Arrange the meat on top of the vegetables in an attractive pattern. Set aside.

3 Dry-fry the sesame seeds in a heavy-based saucepan. Mix together the honey, sherry, soy sauce and water and pour into the pan. Bring to the boil, stirring, then pour over the meat and vegetables. Add salt and pepper to taste. Leave to cool, then cover and marinade in the refrigerator for at least 4 hours. **A** Spoon the marinade over the meat occasionally during this time. Allow to come to room temperature for 30 minutes before serving.

4 Serve with deep-fried prawn crackers and chilled dry white wine for an exotic lunch.

A The meat and vegetables can be left in the marinade overnight.

Frozen spinach is specified in the recipe for spinach and ham crêpes because it is so quick and convenient to use. You may prefer to cook fresh spinach, in which case you will need 450 g (1 lb). Wash it thoroughly, tearing off any thick woody stalks and discarding any yellow or damaged leaves. Place the spinach in a large saucepan with only the water that clings to the leaves and cook over moderate heat for about 8 minutes until tender. Drain thoroughly, then chop finely.

SPINACH AND HAM CRÊPES

Makes 8

100 g (4 oz) plain flour
salt
1 egg, beaten
300 ml (½ pint) milk
450 g (1 lb) frozen chopped spinach (see left)
50 g (2 oz) butter
2 tablespoons soured cream
¼ teaspoon freshly grated nutmeg
freshly ground black pepper
225 g (8 oz) leftover cooked ham or bacon (from a joint), diced
50 g (2 oz) Double Gloucester or Cheddar cheese, grated
vegetable oil, for shallow frying crêpes
Cheese Sauce:
50 g (2 oz) butter
3 tablespoons plain flour
450 ml (¾ pint) milk
175 g (6 oz) Double Gloucester or Cheddar cheese, grated
pinch of ground mace

Preparation time: 50 minutes, plus standing
Cooking time: about 1 hour
Oven: 200°C, 400°F, Gas Mark 6

1 To make the crêpes, sift the flour into a bowl with a pinch of salt. Make a well in the centre and gradually add the eggs and milk. Whisk well to combine to a smooth batter. (Alternatively, mix batter ingredients in a blender or food processor.) Leave the batter to stand for at least 30 minutes.

2 Meanwhile, make the filling. Put the frozen spinach in a heavy-based saucepan and heat gently for 10-15 minutes until thawed. Increase the heat and stir until the spinach is quite dry. Turn off the heat and add the butter, soured cream, nutmeg and salt and pepper to taste. Beat well, then fold in the ham or bacon and the cheese. **A** Keep warm.

3 Make the cheese sauce. Melt the butter in a saucepan, sprinkle in the flour and cook, stirring, for 1-2 minutes. Remove from the heat and beat in the milk a little at a time. Return to the heat and simmer, stirring, until smooth. Stir in half of the cheese, the mace, pepper to taste and salt if necessary. Simmer for a further few minutes until the cheese has melted. Remove the sauce from the heat, cover the surface closely with cling film or buttered greaseproof. **A** Keep warm.

Spinach and Ham Crêpes; Country Noodle Soup

COUNTRY NOODLE SOUP

leftover meat bones

1 onion, peeled and stuck with
a few cloves

2 carrots, peeled and
roughly chopped

2 celery sticks, roughly chopped

2 leeks, trimmed and
roughly chopped

2 teaspoons beef extract

1 bouquet garni

salt

freshly ground black pepper

100-175 g (4-6 oz) meat from a roast
joint, shredded or cut into tiny dice

175 g (6 oz) small soup pasta

2 teaspoons tomato purée

To garnish:

chopped fresh parsley

Preparation time: 15 minutes
Cooking time: 1 hour 20 minutes

1 Put the bones in a large saucepan with 1.5 litres (2½ pints) water. Bring to the boil, then skim off the scum with a slotted spoon.

2 Add the vegetables to the pan with the beef extract, bouquet garni and salt and pepper to taste. Half cover the pan with a lid and simmer for 1 hour.

3 Strain the stock through a fine sieve into a clean pan. **A** Add the meat to the stock with the pasta and tomato purée. **F** Simmer for 10 minutes or until the pasta is tender, stirring occasionally. Taste and adjust the seasoning before serving sprinkled with parsley.

4 Serve for a hearty family lunch with hot bread rolls and butter.

A The finished soup will have less fat if the stock is left to cool, then chilled overnight at this stage. Remove any solidified fat the next day and reheat until bubbling before adding the meat and pasta.

F Omit the pasta, cool and keep in the refrigerator overnight, then remove any solidified fat. Freeze in a rigid container for up to 3 months. Reheat from frozen, adding a little water to prevent the soup sticking to the base of the pan. Add the pasta and cook as above.

4 To make the crêpes, heat a little oil in a pancake pan or heavy-based frying pan. Stir the batter well. Pour one-eighth of the batter into the pan and swirl to cover the base. Cook for 1-2 minutes until the underside is set and golden, then turn the crêpe over and cook for a further 20-30 seconds on the other side. Remove the crêpe from the pan. **A** Spoon one-eighth of the spinach filling in the centre and roll up. Place in a buttered ovenproof serving dish and keep warm.

5 Continue making and filling 8 crêpes, then pour over the cheese sauce and sprinkle with the remaining cheese. **F** Cook in a preheated oven for 15-20 minutes until golden brown and bubbling.

6 Serve the crêpes piping hot with a mixed side salad of tomatoes, watercress, endive and cucumber.

A The crêpes, filling and sauce can all be made up to 24 hours in advance, then the dish assembled before baking. Stack the crêpes on a plate with grease-proof paper between each one.

F Freeze in the dish for up to 2 months. Bake from frozen, allowing an extra 15-20 minutes. (Cover with foil if the topping becomes too brown.)

LUNCHES FOR TEENAGERS

Teenagers won't thank you for sensible food, so how can you strike a balance between food that is 'good for you', and the junk food that they all seem to love? The answer is to tempt their tastebuds by cooking fresh, nutritious ingredients imaginatively and excitingly.

Most children and teenagers have their main meal of the day at lunchtime, so it should be substantial and nutritious. Children tend to be conservative in their tastes in food, so try to keep ingredients familiar, but at the same time dress them up in different guises to prevent boredom setting in. The recipes in this section will give you inspiration to create lunchtime meals which both adults and youngsters will enjoy eating together. Two of the dishes can be eaten with the fingers – always a hit with teenagers – and several of the recipes are for composite dishes which need no accompaniment.

Literally translated, Mozzarella in carrozza means Mozzarella cheese 'in a carriage'. That is, the cheese is 'carried' in between the two slices of bread. The dish is best described as a gooey cheese sandwich (Italian Mozzarella cheese has a wonderful 'stringy' melting quality). This version has tomato ketchup and oregano inside for added interest, so it tastes like a mini pizza. Let the children help to brush the flour and water paste on to the bread.

MOZZARELLA IN CARROZZA

4 medium-thick slices of stale white bread, crusts removed

softened butter, for spreading

salt

freshly ground black pepper

1 × 120 g (4½ oz) packet Italian Mozzarella cheese, sliced

4 teaspoons tomato ketchup

1 teaspoon dried oregano

1 tablespoon flour

1 large egg, beaten

vegetable oil, for shallow-frying

Preparation time: 20 minutes
Cooking time: 2 minutes

1 Cut each slice of bread into one triangle by cutting off wedges from 2 of the sides. Spread one side of each triangle with butter and sprinkle with salt and pepper. Cover 4 of the triangles with slices of Mozzarella, leaving a narrow margin around the edges.

2 Spread 1 teaspoon tomato ketchup over the cheese, then sprinkle each one with ¼ teaspoon oregano. Top with the remaining triangles, butter down. Press firmly.

3 Mix the flour to a paste with a little cold water and brush inside the triangle edges. Press the edges to seal them.

4 Dip the sandwiches in the beaten egg until thoroughly and evenly coated, then shallow fry in hot oil for 1 minute on each side until golden. Drain the sandwiches quickly on paper towels and serve immediately.

FRUITY SPARE RIBS

1-1.25 kg (2-2½ lb) Chinese style pork spare ribs (see right)

150 ml (¼ pint) orange juice

about 150 ml (¼ pint) chicken stock

finely grated rind of 2 oranges

4 tablespoons clear honey

3 tablespoons tomato ketchup

2 tablespoons Worcestershire sauce

salt

freshly ground black pepper

100 g (4 oz) mixed stoned dried fruit, soaked in cold water overnight

Preparation time: 20 minutes, plus overnight soaking
Cooking time: 1½ hours
Oven: 200°C, 400°F, Gas Mark 6

Fruity Spare Ribs (with fingerbowls); Mozzarella in Carrozza

1 Cut the spare ribs into individual chops. Place them in a lightly greased roasting tin. Measure the orange juice and make up to 300 ml (½ pint) with stock. Add the remaining ingredients, except the dried fruit, and stir well.

2 Pour the orange juice mixture over the chops. **A** Roast in a preheated oven for 1 hour, basting occasionally.

3 Drain the dried fruit and chop roughly into bite-sized pieces. Add the fruit to the tin, mixing it into the sauce. Return the tin to the oven and cook for a further 30 minutes or until the chops are well browned. Serve with rice.

4 The chops should be eaten with the fingers (provide finger bowls and plenty of paper napkins too!).

A The chops can be left to marinate for up to 24 hours (in the refrigerator).

STUFFED BAKED POTATOES

4 medium baking potatoes

50 g (2 oz) butter

4 spring onions, trimmed and very finely chopped

6 tablespoons drained canned sweetcorn

1 × 200 g (7 oz) can tuna, drained

salt

freshly ground black pepper

4 tablespoons soured cream

Preparation time: 15 minutes
Cooking time: 1¼ hours
Oven: 200°C, 400°F, Gas Mark 6

1 Scrub the potatoes clean under cold water, then pat dry with paper towels. Pierce holes in the potatoes with a fine skewer, then cook in a preheated oven for 1¼ hours until tender.

2 Towards the end of the cooking time, prepare the filling. Melt half of the butter in a saucepan, add the spring onions and fry gently for 1-2 minutes until slightly softened. Add the sweetcorn and heat through, then add the tuna and toss gently to heat through.

3 Remove the potatoes from the oven. Cut off lids lengthways and scoop out the flesh. Mash the flesh with the remaining butter and salt and pepper to taste, then quickly fold in the tuna fish mixture. Spoon the mixture back into the potato shells and pour 1 tablespoon soured cream over each. Serve immediately.

Chinese or American style spare ribs are available at some large supermarkets, but your family butcher will cut them for you if you tell him precisely what you want. Do not confuse ribs with 'spare rib chops', which are more common. Chinese, or American, ribs are cut from the belly and are usually sold in a rack, whereas spare rib chops are thicker and meatier, cut from the neck end. Ribs must be eaten with the fingers!

Children will love dunking their fish puffs in a tasty home-made tomato mayonnaise dip. Use your own thick mayonnaise if you have time to make it (page 40), otherwise use a good-quality bottled mayonnaise made with fresh eggs. To 150 ml (¼ pint) mayonnaise, add 2 teaspoons tomato purée, 1 skinned and finely chopped tomato, 1 finely chopped spring onion, a pinch of sugar and lemon juice and salt and pepper to taste. Whisk vigorously to combine.

FISH PUFFS

Makes 12

4 frozen (boneless and skinless)
cod or haddock steaks

25 g (1 oz) butter

2 tablespoons plain flour

2 tablespoons grated Parmesan
cheese

4 tablespoons milk

1 egg, separated

salt

freshly ground black pepper

vegetable oil, for deep-frying

To garnish:

lemon slices

fresh parsley or dill

Preparation time: *10-15 minutes*
Cooking time: *6 minutes*

1 Cut each fish steak into 3 equal pieces. Melt the butter in a frying pan, add the fish pieces and fry for 1 minute on each side. Remove with a slotted spoon and leave to cool and drain on paper towels. **A**

2 Meanwhile, put the flour in a large shallow dish with the Parmesan, milk and egg yolk. Add salt and pepper to taste and beat well to mix. **A** Heat the oil in a deep-fat frier to 190°C (375°F).

3 In the meantime, whisk the egg white until stiff. Fold into the egg yolk mixture. Immediately put 6 of the fish pieces into the batter, turning them with a fork to ensure they become well coated.

4 Using the fork, transfer the fish pieces to the hot oil. Deep-fry for 2 minutes, until crisp and golden, turning if necessary. Coat the remaining fish pieces in the batter while the first batch is frying. Remove the fish puffs from the oil with a slotted spoon and drain quickly on paper towels. Serve immediately garnished with lemon slices and parsley or dill.

5 Serve with a tomato mayonnaise dip (see left) and French fries.

A The fish can be fried and left to cool and the batter prepared (*without* the egg white) up to 1 hour in advance. Once the egg white is added to the batter it must be used immediately, in which case the oil should be heated to the required temperature before folding in the whisked egg white.

TOP HAT SOUP

100 g (4 oz) brown rice

50 g (2 oz) butter

1 small onion, peeled and
finely chopped

4 medium carrots, peeled and
finely diced

1 large potato, about 225 g (8 oz)
in weight, peeled and finely diced

225 g (8 oz) split red lentils, rinsed

900 ml (1½ pints) water

1 vegetable stock cube

salt

freshly ground black pepper

1 × 225 g (8 oz) packet frozen
puff pastry, thawed

beaten egg, to glaze

Preparation time: *30 minutes,*
plus cooling
Cooking time: *1 hour 10 minutes*
Oven: *200°C, 400°F, Gas Mark 6*

1 Put the brown rice in a large saucepan, cover with plenty of cold water (no salt) and bring to the boil. Drain and rinse under cold running water.

2 Melt the butter in the rinsed-out pan, add the onion, carrots and potato and cook very gently for 5 minutes. Add the lentils and cook for a further 5 minutes, then add the water and stock cube. Bring to the boil, stirring to dissolve the stock cube.

3 Lower the heat, add the rice, cover the pan and simmer very gently for 20 minutes or until both rice and lentils are cooked. Remove from the heat, add salt and pepper, then leave until cold. **A**

4 Divide the cold soup equally between 4 ovenproof soup bowls with rims. Roll out the pastry on a floured surface and cut out 4 lids to fit the soup bowls (page 7). Cut out 4 strips of pastry long enough to go around the rims of the bowls, then stick the strips on the bowls with water. Brush the pastry strips with more water and press the lids on top.

5 Knock up and flute the edges, make a hole in the centre of each lid and decorate with pastry trimmings. Brush with beaten egg to glaze. **A**

6 Cook on a hot baking sheet in a preheated oven for 30 minutes until the filling is bubbling and the pastry is golden brown. Cover the pastry with foil or greaseproof if it shows signs of over-browning. Leave to cool for about 5 minutes before serving as the soup inside the pastry lid is very hot when first taken from the oven.

7 Serve with grissini (Italian bread sticks) or wholewheat or granary rolls.

A The soup can be made up to 2 days in advance and stored in the refrigerator. Alternatively, make up to the baking stage and keep in a cool place for up to 2 hours.

The combination of brown rice and lentils in top hat soup is extremely nutritious. Lentils are dried pulses, a protein-packed food in themselves, but they do not contain the correct number of amino-acids for a well-balanced healthy diet. When combined with a grain, such as rice, the correct number of amino-acids is obtained – and the result is a balanced nutritious meal.

Top Hat Soup; Fish Puffs with tomato mayonnaise dip

From the top: Pasta Pot; Sausage and Bean Hotpot

The salami sticks in pasta pot are available, individually wrapped in foil, at most large supermarkets. Correctly called peperami in Italian, they are long and thin – and very tasty. An extremely nutritious, high energy food, invented as an easy-to-eat snack for mountaineers, they've now become immensely popular for children's packed lunch boxes at school.

PASTA POT

Serves 2-3

1 × 225 g (8 oz) can tomatoes
1 tablespoon plus 1 teaspoon vegetable oil
½ small onion, peeled and finely chopped
2 teaspoons tomato purée
½ teaspoon sugar
150 ml (¼ pint) vegetable stock or water
salt
freshly ground black pepper
100 g (4 oz) macaroni or other small pasta shapes
300 ml (½ pint) milk
25 g (1 oz) flour
25 g (1 oz) butter
1 egg, beaten
2-3 salami sticks, chopped into bite-sized pieces

Preparation time: *25 minutes*
Cooking time: *40-45 minutes*
Oven: *180°C, 350°F, Gas Mark 4*

1 Put the tomatoes in a blender or food processor with the 1 tablespoon oil, the onion, tomato purée and sugar. Work to a purée, then turn into a saucepan. Add the stock or water and salt and pepper to taste and simmer for 15 minutes, stirring occasionally. **A**
2 Meanwhile, cook the macaroni in plenty of boiling salted water (to which the remaining 1 teaspoon oil has been added) according to packet instructions until *al dente*. **A** Drain thoroughly.
3 Put the milk, flour and butter in the blender or food processor and work for 1 minute to combine. Turn into a saucepan and bring to the boil, then simmer for 5 minutes, stirring until thickened. Remove from the heat, leave to cool for 1-2 minutes, then beat in the egg with salt and pepper to taste.
4 Fold the chopped salami into the tomato sauce, then fold in the pasta. Turn into an ovenproof dish and pour the white sauce over the top. **A** Cook in a preheated oven for 15-20 minutes until bubbling. Serve hot. A mixed green salad is a good accompaniment. **A** The tomato sauce and macaroni can be cooked up to 24 hours in advance and folded together with the salami. Alternatively, the whole dish can be assembled prior to baking and kept in the refrigerator for up to 24 hours.

SAUSAGE AND BEAN HOTPOT

Serves 2-3

350 g (12 oz) potatoes, peeled and halved if large
salt
2 tablespoons vegetable oil
8-12 pork cocktail sausages
2-3 lean bacon rashers, rinded and chopped
1 small onion, peeled and finely chopped
1 × 450 g (1 lb) can baked beans in tomato sauce
150 ml (¼ pint) water
2 tablespoons black treacle
2 teaspoons soy sauce
1 teaspoon French mustard
freshly ground black pepper
15 g (½ oz) butter
1 tablespoon milk
1 small egg, beaten
25-50 g (1-2 oz) cheese, grated

Preparation time: *20 minutes*
Cooking time: *45 minutes*

1 Cook the potatoes in boiling salted water for about 20 minutes until tender. Meanwhile, heat the oil in a large, heavy-based saucepan, add the sausages and fry for about 10 minutes until browned on all sides. Remove with a slotted spoon and drain on paper towels. Add the bacon to the pan and fry until crisp. Remove and drain with the sausages.
2 Add the onion to the pan and fry gently for 5 minutes until soft. Add the beans, water, black treacle, soy sauce, mustard and salt and pepper to taste and heat through, stirring. Add the sausages and bacon and heat through gently.
3 Drain the potatoes and mash with the butter and milk. Beat in the egg with salt and pepper to taste.
4 Turn the sausage and bean mixture into a flameproof dish. Spread the mashed potato over the top. Sprinkle the potato with cheese. **A** Put under a preheated grill until the cheese is golden and bubbling. Serve hot.
5 This dish is substantial enough to need no accompaniment.
A The whole dish can be prepared several hours in advance (or the night before), then cooked from cold in a preheated 200°C, 400°F, Gas Mark 6 oven for 30 minutes.

PORTABLE LUNCHES

Whether it is for a picnic, a packed school lunch or a snack at the office desk, a portable meal needs special care and thought if it is to taste as fresh and delicious as when it was first prepared.

The recipes in this section are for dishes that can be eaten hot, but which will also keep and travel well and retain their taste. Pizza, for instance, was first created in Naples and was an original 'take-away' meal. Bakers made pizzas to use up the dough left over from baking bread and they were bought for a quick, tasty snack often eaten along the street. Nowadays there seems to be a *pizzaria* on every street corner in Italy, and pizzas have become genuine 'fast-food'. Left to go cold and cut into manageable-sized pieces to eat with the fingers, pizza is an excellent picnic food.

Wrapping and packing is all-important with portable food. Foil and cling film are perfect for packing individual portions and preserving freshness. Rigid containers provide added protection, and are a must with fragile foods or items that need to preserve their good looks. It's well worth taking time over packing portable food or the culinary efforts will have been in vain.

Herb and Bean Pâté; Pizza Squares

Making pizza dough at home with fresh yeast is simple to do. If you find that fresh yeast is difficult to obtain, you can of course use dried yeast. For this recipe you will need 15 g (½ oz) dried yeast, which should be dissolved in the 4 tablespoons lukewarm milk with 1 teaspoon caster sugar. If you are short of time, then a short-cut method of making pizza dough is to use packet white bread mix.

PIZZA SQUARES

Makes 20-24 squares
25 g (1 oz) fresh yeast
about 200 ml (⅓ pint) lukewarm milk
400 g (14 oz) strong white bread flour
2 teaspoons salt
3 tablespoons olive or vegetable oil
1 × 400 g (14 oz) can tomatoes, drained with 3 tablespoons juice reserved
1 tablespoon tomato purée
2 teaspoons dried oregano
salt
freshly ground black pepper
1 × 200 g (7 oz) can tuna fish, in oil or brine, drained
1 × 50 g (2 oz) can anchovies in oil, drained and soaked in milk for 20 minutes
100 g (4 oz) Cheddar cheese, grated
about 10 black olives, stoned

Preparation time: 50 minutes, plus soaking, rising, proving and cooling
Cooking time: 20-25 minutes
Oven: 220°C, 425°F, Gas Mark 7

1 Crumble the yeast into 4 tablespoons of the milk in a bowl. Blend together, then leave in a warm place for 10-15 minutes until frothy.

2 Sift 4 tablespoons of the flour into the frothy yeast mixture and stir to mix. Cover and leave again in a warm place until frothy, this time for about 30 minutes.

3 Sift the remaining flour into a large bowl with the salt. Add the yeast mixture, the remaining milk and 2 tablespoons of the oil. Mix to a soft dough, then turn out on to a floured surface and knead for 10 minutes until smooth and elastic. Add the remaining oil during kneading.

4 Put the dough in a floured bowl, cover and return to the warm place. Leave for about 1½ hours until doubled in bulk. **A**

5 Meanwhile, purée the tomatoes and reserved juice in an electric blender or food processor with the tomato purée, half the oregano, salt and pepper.

6 Turn the dough out on to a floured surface and roll into a rectangle to fit a 28 × 23 cm (11 × 9 inch) roasting tin. Place the dough in the oiled tin and pinch the edges to raise them slightly.

7 Mash the tuna fish with a fork and spread over the dough, right to the edges. Spread the tomato mixture over the tuna fish. Drain the milk from the anchovies, pat them dry with a paper towel and cut each one in half. Arrange diagonally on top of the pizza, then sprinkle with the cheese and add the olives. Finally sprinkle with the remaining oregano. Leave to prove for 30 minutes. **F**

8 Place the pizza in a preheated oven and cook for 20-25 minutes until risen and bubbling. Leave to cool for 5 minutes, then cut into 20-24 squares. Leave to cool completely in the tin before removing. **A**

A The dough can be left to rise in the refrigerator overnight. Alternatively, the pizza can be prepared and baked up to 24 hours in advance. Cover the tin with foil or cling film after cooling.

F Open freeze the unbaked pizza until solid, then remove from the tin and wrap in foil. Cook from frozen, allowing an extra 15 minutes.

HERB AND BEAN PÂTÉ

1 × 425 g (15 oz) can cannellini beans, well drained
1 garlic clove, peeled and chopped
finely grated rind of ½ lemon
2 tablespoons lemon juice
100 g (4 oz) butter or margarine, melted
2 teaspoons chopped fresh thyme
2 teaspoons chopped fresh parsley
salt
freshly ground black pepper
To garnish:
sprigs of fresh thyme

Preparation time: 20 minutes, plus chilling

1 Purée the beans and their liquid in an electric blender or food processor with the garlic and lemon rind and juice.

2 Add the butter or margarine, the herbs and salt and pepper to taste. Work again until evenly combined.

3 Turn the pâté into one serving bowl or individual pots or ramekins. **A** Garnish with the thyme sprigs. Cover with cling film and chill in the refrigerator for at least 1 hour. Serve chilled or cold.

A The pâté can be made up to 3 days in advance and stored in the refrigerator.

The spicy patties in pitta parcels are a variation of falafel, one of Israel's most popular 'convenience' foods. In Israel, falafel are usually made with chick-peas and no meat; they are sold on street corners as a quick snack. Packed into warm pitta bread with salad, they make a perfect portable food. For picnics, let the patties go cold before putting them into the pitta with the salad. They will keep fresh for several hours if you wrap them in foil.

PITTA PARCELS

Makes 8
100 g (4 oz) chick peas,
soaked in cold water overnight

100 g (4 oz) lean minced beef

50 g (2 oz) fresh wholewheat breadcrumbs

1 small onion, peeled and finely chopped

1 garlic clove, peeled and crushed

2 teaspoons chopped fresh coriander

1 teaspoon ground cumin

dash of Tabasco sauce

2 small (size 3 or 4) eggs, beaten

salt

freshly ground black pepper

2-3 tablespoons flour, for coating

vegetable oil, for shallow frying

To serve

salad ingredients (such as lettuce leaves, slices of tomato and cucumber, watercress sprigs, spring onions)

4 pitta breads, warmed

Preparation time: 30 minutes, plus overnight soaking, and chilling
Cooking time: about 1 hour 10 minutes

1 Drain the chick peas, rinse under cold running water, then place in a large saucepan and cover with fresh cold water. Bring to the boil, then lower the heat, cover and simmer for 1 hour or until the chick peas are tender.

2 Drain the chick peas and reserve 3 tablespoons of the cooking liquid. Leave to cool slightly, then work the chick peas and liquid in an electric blender or food processor until smooth. Add the minced beef, breadcrumbs, onion, garlic, coriander, cumin and Tabasco. Work again until evenly combined.

3 Bind the mixture with half of the beaten eggs and add salt and pepper to taste. Chill in the refrigerator for at least 30 minutes to firm the mixture.

4 With floured hands, form the mixture into 8 patties. Dip in the remaining beaten egg, then coat in the remaining flour. Chill in the refrigerator for a further 30 minutes. **A**

5 Pour oil into a frying pan to a depth of 2.5 cm (1 inch). Heat until very hot, then fry the patties for about 3 minutes on each side until golden brown. Drain on paper towels. **A** Use with the salad

ingredients to fill 4 warm pitta breads. Cut in half to serve.

A The patties can be made to the frying stage and kept in the refrigerator for 1 or 2 hours until ready to cook. Alternatively, if serving cold, prepare and cook up to 4 hours in advance.

PASTA SALAD

Serves 6
1 teaspoon vegetable oil

salt

300 g (11 oz) pasta shells

350 g (12 oz) French beans

350 g (12 oz) young carrots

8 tablespoons olive oil

2 tablespoons wine vinegar

1 garlic clove, peeled and crushed

2 tablespoons chopped fresh parsley

freshly ground black pepper

3 tablespoons mayonnaise

175 g (6 oz) piece garlic sausage, skinned and diced

175 g (6 oz) Feta cheese, diced

Preparation time: 20 minutes, plus cooling and chilling
Cooking time: 10-15 minutes

1 Bring a large pan of water to the boil, swirl in the oil, then add 1 teaspoon salt. Add the pasta, bring back to the boil and simmer for 10 minutes or according to packet instructions until *al dente* (tender but firm to the bite).

2 Meanwhile, top and tail the French beans and cut them into 2.5 cm (1 inch) lengths. Scrape the carrots and cut into thin matchstick strips. Blanch in boiling water for 3 minutes until tender but still crunchy. Drain the pasta, beans and carrots.

3 Put the oil, wine vinegar, garlic and parsley in a large bowl with salt and pepper to taste. Whisk with a fork to combine, then add the warm pasta and vegetables and toss gently to mix. Leave to cool. **A**

4 Fold the mayonnaise into the salad, then the garlic sausage and cheese. Taste and adjust seasoning, cover with cling film and chill in the refrigerator for at least 1 hour. **A** Serve chilled or cold.

A The pasta, vegetables and dressing mixed together up to 24 hours in advance and chilled. Alternatively, the whole salad can be made up to 4 hours in advance and chilled.

From left to right: Pitta Parcels; Pasta Salad

Spicy Wholesome Cake; Crunchy Chicken Pieces

SPICY WHOLESOME FRUIT CAKE

225 g (8 oz) stoned dates,
roughly chopped

275 ml (9 fl oz) bottle sweet stout

225 g (8 oz) large raisins

100 g (4 oz) soft brown sugar

1 tablespoon molasses or
black treacle

200 g (7 oz) plain white flour

200 g (7 oz) plain wholewheat flour

2 teaspoons ground mixed spice

4 tablespoons vegetable oil

2 eggs, beaten

1 teaspoon bicarbonate of soda
dissolved in 2 teaspoons milk

*Preparation time: 20 minutes,
plus overnight standing and cooling*
Cooking time: 2 hours
Oven: 160°C, 325°F, Gas Mark 3

1 Put the dates in a bowl, pour in the stout and stir well to mix. Cover and leave to stand overnight.

2 The next day, add the raisins, sugar and molasses or treacle to the dates and stir until the sugar has dissolved. Sift in the flours and mixed spice, then tip in any bran remaining in the sieve from the wholewheat flour. Beat well to mix, then add the oil, eggs and soda and milk mixture. Beat again until all the ingredients are evenly combined.

3 Spoon the mixture into a greased and base-lined 20 cm (8 inch) round cake tin. **A** Place in a preheated oven and bake for 2 hours or until a skewer inserted in the centre comes out clean. Leave to cool in the tin for 10-15 minutes, then turn out and leave to cool completely on a wire tray. **A**

A The cake mixture can be left for up to 24 hours before baking if more convenient.

Wrapped in cling film or foil and stored in an airtight tin, the finished cake will keep fresh for up to 1 week.

If you prefer, you can use tea instead of stout for soaking the dates in this recipe. Make medium-strength tea in the pot as usual, leave until cold, then strain before use. Ordinary China or Indian blends of tea can be used, but if you would like the cake to have a slightly perfumed flavour (which would go well with the mixed spice), then use Earl Grey or Lapsang Souchong.

CRUNCHY CHICKEN PIECES

Makes 6
*6 chicken breast fillets,
each weighing 50-75 g (2-3 oz)*
100 g (4 oz) firm pâté or liver sausage
*50 g (2 oz) button mushrooms,
wiped and finely chopped*
salt
freshly ground black pepper
1½ tablespoons flour
1 large egg, beaten
75 g (3 oz) fresh breadcrumbs
1½ teaspoons dried mixed herbs
¼ teaspoon English mustard powder
vegetable oil, for deep-frying

Preparation time: *1 hour,
plus chilling*
Cooking time: *10-15 minutes,
plus cooling*

1 Remove the skin from the chicken breasts and open the flesh out flat. Place between 2 sheets of greaseproof paper and beat out gently with a meat mallet or rolling pin. Set aside.

2 Mash the pâté with a fork in a bowl, then add the mushrooms and work them into the pâté until evenly combined. Add salt and pepper to taste.

3 Place a little of the pâté and mushroom mixture in the centre of each chicken breast, then roll the chicken up around it.

4 Coat in the flour seasoned with salt and pepper, then dip in the beaten egg. Mix the breadcrumbs, herbs and mustard together, then use to coat the chicken breasts. Secure with wooden cocktail sticks, if necessary. Chill in the refrigerator for at least 30 minutes.

5 Heat the oil in a deep-fat frier to 180°C (350°F), then deep-fry the chicken breasts for 10-15 minutes, turning them constantly, until the coating is golden brown and crisp. Drain on paper towels. Leave to cool, then pack in a rigid container and store in the refrigerator. **A** Serve cold with tomatoes and watercress.

A Prepare and cook completely the night before, leave to cool, then keep in the refrigerator.

CHEESE AND NUT LOAF

Serves 6-8
2 tablespoons vegetable oil
*1 small onion, peeled and
finely chopped*
1 celery stick, finely chopped
2 dessert apples, cored and grated
15 g (½ oz) butter
*2-3 teaspoons garam masala
(see right)*
*75 g (3 oz) crustless stale granary
breadcrumbs*
*175 g (6 oz) shelled mixed nuts,
roughly chopped*
*120 g (4½ oz) Double Gloucester or
Red Leicester cheese, grated*
1 egg, beaten
2 tablespoons tomato ketchup
salt
freshly ground black pepper
*good pinch of paprika or cayenne,
to finish*

Preparation time: *40 minutes,
plus cooling*
Cooking time: *40 minutes*
Oven: *180°C, 350°F, Gas Mark 4*

1 Heat the oil in a small pan, add the onion and celery and fry gently until soft. Add the grated apple, butter, garam masala and fry for a further 2-3 minutes, stirring constantly.

2 Turn the mixture into a bowl and add the breadcrumbs, nuts and 100 g (4 oz) of the cheese. Mix well, then add the egg, tomato ketchup and salt and pepper to taste. Work again until all the ingredients are evenly combined.

3 Spoon the mixture into a greased and base-lined 450 g (1 lb) loaf tin. Press the mixture down well, then mound the centre slightly to give a loaf shape.

4 Place the loaf in a preheated oven and bake for 30 minutes until firm, then sprinkle with the remaining cheese and the paprika or cayenne. (Use cayenne more sparingly.) Return to the oven for a further 5 minutes. Leave to cool in the tin for 30 minutes. Turn the loaf out and cool on a wire tray before slicing and wrapping in cling film. **A** **F**

A The loaf can be made up to 3 days in advance, wrapped in cling film and stored in the refrigerator.

F Overwrap in a polythene bag and freeze for up to 1 month. Defrost the loaf in the wrappings in the refrigerator overnight.

Garam masala is used frequently in Indian cookery. Ready-mixed garam masala is available from Indian specialist shops, delicatessens and supermarkets, but these mixtures often taste stale as the essential oils of the spices do not keep fresh for long. To ensure maximum flavour it is best to make your own garam masala as and when you need it. Grind together the seeds from 4 black cardamoms, 1 tablespoon black peppercorns, 4 teaspoons coriander seeds, 2 teaspoons cumin seeds and 1 teaspoon cloves. Store in an airtight container, but use as soon as possible.

Michael Smith
CELEBRITY COOK

Lunch can be one of the most enjoyable meals of the day whether it's a brief halt in a busy day or a leisurely weekend affair that drifts on, like the conversation of the guests, well into the late afternoon.

My favourite place to eat lunch is my garden, on a paved area where I have a table and six plump-cushioned armchairs (the perfect number and shape for good conversation). I have jade-green cotton cloths and napkins, simple white china, a side table (essential for serving from and clearing to) and a vast umbrella against sun – or drizzle!

So that I can enjoy lunch too, I plan a menu which requires me to move no more than once from the table during the meal. I choose chilled soups – and I mean really chilled by turning the fridge up overnight and chilling the soup dishes as well. Choose red pepper and ginger soup or creamy curried courgette soup followed by an imaginative cheeseboard (try including a home-made fruity bread). A composite salad such as England's solomongundy – makes a handsome lunch served on a vast platter from which friends can help themselves. I have also included two desserts in my choice of recipes – a roman cheesecake and a rice pudding ice cream – both equally irresistible.

Prawn and Avocado Salad; Special Shepherd's Pie

To enrich the mince itself in this special shepherd's pie add a crushed clove of garlic and half a head of celery, finely sliced and fried at the same time as the onions. I have been known to use instant mashed potato on occasions which, when reconstituted and beaten with the other topping ingredients is unbelievably good.

SPECIAL SHEPHERD'S PIE

1½ tablespoons olive oil and/or butter for frying

225 g (8 oz) onions, peeled and finely chopped

750 kg (1½ lb) best minced lamb (page 40)

1 tablespoons tomato purée

15 g (½ oz) flour

salt

freshly ground black pepper

450 ml (¾ pint) stock, water or half red wine, half water

bouquet garni

Topping:

750 g (1½ lb) potatoes, peeled, cooked and well mashed

65 ml (2½ fl oz) double cream, gently heated with 25 g (1 oz) butter

½ teaspoon grated nutmeg

Optional extras:

450 g (1 lb) tomatoes, sliced

225 g (8 oz) mushrooms, sliced, seasoned and fried in 25 g (1 oz) butter

75 g (3 oz) grated Dutch cheese

Preparation time: 10 minutes
Cooking time: 1½-2 hours
Oven: 180°C, 350°F, Gas Mark 4; then 200°C, 400°F, Gas Mark 6

1 Place oil and/or butter in a large heavy-based flameproof casserole and fry the onions until golden, stirring. Remove onions and fry the mince in batches, until browned.

2 Return the first batches of meat and the onions to the pan and mix well. Add the tomato purée and mix well. Sprinkle over the flour and salt and pepper. Stir in the stock, water or wine mixture and add the bouquet garni.

3 Cover, place in a preheated oven (at the lower temperature) and cook for 1 hour. Leave to cool. Skim off excess fat.

4 To make the topping, mix the ingredients together, adding salt and pepper. Cover or pipe the meat mixture with the potato topping, return the pie to the oven, uncovered and cook at the higher oven temperature for about 15 minutes until hot, brown and bubbling.

5 If using the extras, add a layer of tomatoes and/or mushrooms *before* the topping. Add the cheese, half before and half after the topping. With any of these extras the pie should be cooked for at least an extra half-hour at the lower temperature.

PRAWN AND AVOCADO SALAD

Serves 4-6

½ cucumber

2 avocado pears

1 lemon

1 chicken stock cube

225-275 g (8-10 oz) small cauliflower florets

100 g (4 oz) mange-tout, stringed

2 oranges, peeled and segmented

450 g (1 lb) Mediterranean prawns, shelled (retain 4-6 unshelled)

Dressing:

1 teaspoon mustard powder

1 clove garlic, peeled and crushed

1 teaspoon finely grated orange rind

150 ml (¼ pint) olive oil

2 tablespoons wine vinegar

1 teaspoon caster sugar

¼ teaspoon white pepper

¼ teaspoon salt

To garnish:

1 tablespoon chopped fresh chives or parsley

1 bunch of watercress

lettuce (optional)

Preparation time: 15 minutes, plus chilling
Cooking time: 5 minutes

1 Take alternate strips of rind off the cucumber with a canelle knife. Cut in half lengthways, discard the seeds and cut into 5 mm (¼ inch) thick pieces.

2 Peel the avocados and remove the stones. Cut into 5 mm (¼ inch) thick strips lengthways and toss them in about 3 tablespoons lemon juice.

3 Use the stock cube to make 900 ml (1½ pints) of chicken stock, adding 1½ tablespoons lemon juice and the lemon shell. Cook the cauliflower florets for 1½ minutes in the boiling stock, remove with a slotted spoon and cool.

4 Cook the mange-tout in the stock for 2 minutes, remove and cool under running cold water. Drain.

5 Make the dressing by shaking all the ingredients in a screw-top jar.

6 Put the dressing and salad ingredients (stored in separate plastic bags) in the refrigerator to chill.

7 Just before serving, gently toss everything together in a large bowl. Scoop into dishes, lined with lettuce (if used). Spoon over the dressing, sprinkle with chives or parsley and garnish with watercress and an unshelled prawn.

It took me some time before I really came to terms with using red peppers other than as a crunchy part of a salad or crudités. I'm now addicted to their fruity deep-toned sweetness and this recipe uses them to great effect.

RED PEPPER AND GINGER SOUP

Serves 4-6

100 g (4 oz) butter

4 large red peppers, seeded and roughly chopped

2 large leeks (mostly white part only), roughly chopped and washed

2 teaspoons ground ginger

3 teaspoons sweet paprika

1 tablespoon caster sugar

1 teaspoon sea salt

1 teaspoon white pepper

rind of 1 large orange

4 tablespoons orange juice

600 ml (1 pint) strong chicken stock

600 ml (1 pint) buttermilk or plain unsweetened yogurt

To serve:

4 tablespoons flaked almonds

a little oil and butter, for frying

Preparation time: 10 minutes, plus chilling
Cooking time: about 35 minutes

1 Melt the butter in a saucepan without browning. Add the peppers and leeks, cover and cook over a low heat to soften, stirring occasionally.

2 Add the remaining ingredients except the buttermilk or yogurt. Simmer for 30 minutes. Cool, blend to a fine purée. Chill.

3 Stir in the buttermilk or yogurt. Chill again.

4 Lightly fry the almonds in oil and butter. Serve the soup in chilled bowls with the almonds sprinkled over.

CURRIED COURGETTE SOUP

Serves 6-8

1 kg (2 lb) medium courgettes

50 g (2 oz) butter

2 tablespoons arachid or olive oil

100 g (4 oz) spring onions, trimmed and washed with 2.5 cm (1 inch) of green left on, and roughly chopped

1 teaspoon mild curry powder

1 teaspoon ground cumin powder

1 teaspoon grated orange rind

450 ml (¾ pint) chicken stock

salt

freshly ground black pepper

600 ml (1 pint) buttermilk or plain unsweetened yogurt

To garnish:

1 or 2 oranges

Preparation time: 15 minutes, plus chilling
Cooking time: about 25 minutes

1 Wash, top and tail the courgettes, taking off a little of the skin in alternate strips with a potato peeler. Cut them into discs 5 mm (¼ inch) thick.

2 Melt the butter and oil in a large pan. Add the courgettes and onions and soften them over a low heat for about 15 minutes, stirring to avoid any browning. Add the curry powder and cumin and cook for a further 2-3 minutes, stirring from time to time. Add the orange rind, then pour in the stock and simmer for a further 3 minutes. Add salt and pepper to taste.

3 Cool, then blend thoroughly to a fine purée. Transfer the purée to a large bowl and stir in the buttermilk or yogurt. Taste and adjust the seasoning, cover with plastic film and chill for 4-5 hours, or overnight.

4 Adjust the consistency with a little chilled chicken stock if necessary. Serve in chilled soup bowls, garnished with 2 or 3 thin orange slices.

SOLOMONGUNDY

1 cold cooked chicken (either pot-roast or boiled)

1 lettuce, washed and shredded

12 button onions, skinned

1 × 225 g (8 oz) packet frozen whole green beans

1 × 50 g (2 oz) tin anchovy fillets

100 g (4 oz) black or green grapes, peeled and seeded

4 hard-boiled eggs, shelled and quartered

50 g (2 oz) flaked almonds

50 g (2 oz) stoned raisins

Dressing:

3 tablespoons olive oil

1 tablespoon red or white wine vinegar

1 tablespoon lemon juice

1 teaspoon salt

1 teaspoon finely chopped or grated lemon rind

1 teaspoon flower blossom honey

1 teaspoon mild French mustard

½ garlic clove, peeled and crushed (optional)

1 tablespoon mixed chopped fresh herbs (choose not more than 2 types, e.g. mint, golden marjoram, chives)

Never has a dish had so many different spellings. This English salad is Britain's answer to France's salad Niçoise and is well enough known as a joke because of its extraordinary name. Perhaps saladmagundi will give a better clue to what is a truly excellent salad which, once tried, will never be allowed again to sink into oblivion. This salad has been with us since Tudor times, but for reasons which no-one can explain it has been forgotten for decades.

Preparation time: *30 minutes*
Cooking time: *about 15 minutes,*

1 Skin the chicken and carve the breasts and legs into thin slices.
2 Arrange the lettuce on a large flat platter. Cook the onions in boiling water until just tender.
3 Plunge the beans into boiling salted water for 2 minutes, rinse under run-ning cold water until they are cold, and drain thoroughly on paper towels.
4 To make the dressing put all the ingredients in a screw-topped jar and shake to mix thoroughly.
5 Arrange all the salad items in attractive groups on the bed of lettuce. Pour over the dressing and when ready to serve the salad, toss everything together.

*Clockwise from top:
Solomongundy; Red
Pepper and Ginger
Soup; Curried
Courgette Soup*

35

ROMAN CHEESECAKE

Serves 6

Pastry base (optional):

350 g (12 oz) frozen shortcrust pastry, thawed	
or home-made pastry using:	
75 g (3 oz) butter	
50 g (2 oz) lard	
200 g (7 oz) flour	
1 teaspoon icing sugar	
2 tablespoons cold water for mixing	

Filling:

100 g (4 oz) unsalted butter
225 g (8 oz) caster sugar
450 g (1 lb) full fat soft cheese
2 tablespoons flower blossom honey
120 ml (4 fl oz) single cream
1 teaspoon vanilla essence
5 eggs, separated
50 g (2 oz) plain flour, sifted
100 g (4 oz) flaked almonds

Topping:

50 g (2 oz) soft brown sugar
1 teaspoon cinnamon
50 g (2 oz) flaked almonds

To decorate:

sieved icing sugar

*Preparation time: 15 minutes,
plus making pastry
Cooking time: 1 hour
Oven: 160°C, 325°F, Gas Mark 3*

1 To make the home-made pastry, rub the fats into the flour until the mixture resembles breadcrumbs. Add the icing sugar and combine with enough cold water to mix into a dough.

2 Use the shortcrust or home-made pastry to line a lightly buttered 25 cm (10 inch) spring form tin. (It is not essential to line the spring form with pastry for this recipe, it is optional.) Put the lined tin into the freezer or refrigerator for 30 minutes while you make up the filling.

3 Cream the butter and sugar until light and fluffy. Add the soft cheese and beat well. Add the honey, cream, vanilla essence, egg yolks and flour. Mix well. Beat the egg whites until stiff and lightly fold into the mixture together with the flaked almonds.

4 Pour into the pastry case (or into a well buttered unlined tin) and sprinkle evenly with the topping ingredients. Place in a preheated oven and cook for 1 hour, then turn off the heat and allow to cool in the oven to prevent the mixture coming away from the pastry. Dredge with sieved icing sugar to decorate and serve with thick, unsweetened cream.

RICE-PUDDING ICE CREAM

Serves 8

75 g (3 oz) short grain (pudding) rice
600 ml (1 pint) milk
175 g (6 oz) caster sugar
50 ml (2 fl oz) water
450 ml (¾ pint) double cream

*Preparation time: about 15 minutes,
plus churning or freezing
Cooking time: about 50 minutes*

1 In a double boiler gently cook the rice and milk, with 50 g (2 oz) of the sugar, for 45 minutes, stirring from time to time.

2 Bring the remaining sugar and water to the boil. Boil rapidly for about 3 minutes, or until thick and syrupy, and the syrup makes a soft ball (or reaches 115°C, 238°F on a sugar thermometer). Stir into the hot rice mixture. Allow to cool completely.

3 Stir in the double cream. Put into an ice cream maker and follow the manufacturer's instructions to complete. Alternatively, put into a container and freeze. Every half hour turn the mixture out into a bowl and beat with a wooden spoon until creamy. Return the mixture to the freezer. Repeat this process 2 or 3 times, every half hour, until the ice cream is smooth.

4 Transfer the ice cream to the refrigerator for about half an hour before serving. Scoop into glasses and serve with ice cream wafers.

Variations:
Halfway through churning or freezing, before the ice-cream starts to set, stir in any combination of the following:
2 tablespoons light rum
100 g (4 oz) seedless raisins, plumped up in hot water and drained well
100 g (4 oz) fresh soft citrus peel, finely chopped
50 g (2 oz) ground almonds.

*Roman Cheesecake;
Rice-Pudding Ice
Cream*

SUMMER LUNCHES

Summer is a splendid season for fresh ingredients. There is a wide choice, from soft summer fruits for sumptuous desserts through to crisp and crunchy vegetables. You'll be able to grow or buy fresh herbs to add to recipes – and introduce simple accompaniments from the array of salad produce available.

To take advantage of good weather, and not waste precious hours indoors in the kitchen, try to prepare ingredients in the cool of the night before, or in the early part of the morning, and eat outside whenever you can. If you have a barbecue you can also do most of the cooking outside, which makes the whole exercise pleasurable and sociable.

TOMATO AND ANCHOVY QUICHES

225 g (8 oz) frozen shortcrust
pastry, thawed

2 eggs (size 1)

50 g (2 oz) grated Parmesan cheese

150 ml (¼ pint) double cream

2 teaspoons chopped fresh basil
or 1 teaspoon dried basil

salt

freshly ground black pepper

4 ripe medium tomatoes, skinned
and finely chopped

4 canned anchovy fillets,
soaked in milk for 20 minutes

2 black olives, stoned and halved

*Preparation time: 30 minutes,
plus soaking and standing
Cooking time: 35-40 minutes,
Oven: 200°C, 400°F, Gas Mark 6;
then 180°C, 350°F, Gas Mark 4*

1 Roll out the pastry on a floured surface and use to line 4 individual 13 cm (5 inch) quiche tins. Prick the bases with a fork, then line with foil and baking beans. Place in a preheated oven and bake 'blind' for 10 minutes, then remove the foil and beans and bake for a further 5 minutes until the pastry is cooked. **A**

2 Put the eggs in a bowl with the Parmesan, cream, basil and salt and pepper to taste. (Add only a little salt because of the saltiness of the Parmesan, anchovies and olives.) Beat lightly.

3 Divide the tomatoes between the pastry cases. Slowly pour in the egg and cream mixture. Drain the anchovies and pat dry with paper towels. Cut each anchovy in half lengthways, then arrange 2 anchovy halves in a criss-cross pattern on top of each quiche. Place an olive half in the centre, then stand the quiche tins on a hot baking sheet. Reduce the oven temperature and bake for 20-25 minutes until the filling is just set. **F** Leave for 15 minutes before removing from the quiche tins.

4 Serve warm or cold with a green salad of watercress and curly endive tossed in walnut oil vinaigrette dressing and sprinkled with a few finely chopped walnuts.

A Make pastry cases up to 2 days in advance and store in an airtight tin.

F When cold, open freeze until solid and remove from the tins. Wrap individually in foil and freeze for up to 1 month.

CREAMY ANDALUSIAN GAZPACHO

Serves 8

8 ripe large tomatoes,
roughly chopped

1 small cucumber, roughly chopped

2 ripe red peppers, cored,
seeded and roughly chopped

1 thick slice of white bread,
crusts removed

2 garlic cloves, peeled and
roughly chopped

4 tablespoons thick mayonnaise

¼ teaspoon chilli powder

900 ml (1½ pints) ice-cold
vegetable stock

salt

freshly ground black pepper

*Preparation time: 40 minutes,
plus chilling*

1 Liquidize the tomatoes, cucumber and peppers in batches in an electric blender or food processor. Sieve to remove skin and seeds, then return to the rinsed-out blender or food processor. Crumble in the bread, then work again until smooth. Pour into a bowl and chill for 45 minutes.

2 Crush the garlic with a mortar and pestle, then work in the mayonnaise and chilli powder. Add a few spoonfuls of the puréed vegetables, working them gradually until smooth. Transfer to a large bowl and gradually whisk in the remaining puréed vegetables, then the vegetable stock.

3 Liquidize the mixture again in the blender or food processor until very smooth, then add salt and pepper to taste and thin down with ice-cold water if the consistency is too thick. Pour into a large serving bowl and chill for at least 1 hour before serving. **A** **F**

4 Serve the gazpacho chilled with bowls of finely chopped hard-boiled egg, cucumber, red pepper, tomato and tiny toasted croûtons which guests can sprinkle over their individual servings.

A Make up to 24 hours in advance and chill. Whisk before serving and thin down the consistency with ice-cold water if necessary.

F Freeze in a rigid container for up to 1 month. Defrost overnight in the refrigerator, then whisk vigorously (or work in a blender or food processor) before serving. Thin down with ice-cold water if necessary.

There are many variations of the Spanish iced soup gazpacho, according to the region where it is made. Most recipes from central and northern Spain are a rich red with an acidic flavour which comes from the vinegar used. Andalusian gazpacho is paler in colour and creamy in flavour. One thing it does have in common with other gazpacho soups is the heady flavour of garlic – so do not decrease the quantity if you want the soup to taste authentic.

Tomato and Anchovy Quiche; Creamy Andalusian Gazpacho with accompaniments

Minced lamb is available pre-packed from the chilling cabinets of some large supermarkets. Alternatively, buy boned shoulder of lamb and ask your butcher to mince it or mince it yourself. It is important that a fatty rather than a lean meat is used in this recipe, to ensure succulent and juicy kebabs.

SEEKH KEBABS

Serves 4-6

2 teaspoons coriander seeds

2 teaspoons cumin seeds

2 black peppercorns

seeds of 2 cardamoms

2 cloves

1 small onion, peeled and finely chopped

1 garlic clove, peeled and crushed

2.5 cm (1 inch) piece fresh root ginger, peeled and chopped

2 whole green chillies, seeds removed and finely chopped

750 g (1½ lb) minced lamb

1 teaspoon chilli powder

salt

1 egg, beaten

2 tablespoons plain flour

4 tablespoons vegetable oil

Raita Sauce:

150 ml (¼ pint) plain unsweetened yogurt

¼ cucumber, roughly chopped

2 teaspoons mint jelly

freshly ground black pepper

Preparation time: *30 minutes, plus chilling*
Cooking time: *about 10-11 minutes*

1 Put the coriander and cumin seeds in a small frying pan with the peppercorns, cardamom seeds and cloves. Dry-fry for a few minutes, shaking the pan constantly. Remove from the pan and grind in a mortar and pestle. Put the onion, garlic, ginger, chillies and ground spices into a blender or food processor and work until evenly mixed.

2 Add the lamb in batches, half the chilli powder and ½ teaspoon salt and work again until mixed. Transfer the mixture into a bowl and stir thoroughly with the egg until evenly combined. Chill in the refrigerator for at least 30 minutes.

3 With floured hands, shape the mixture into about 16 'cork' shapes and coat in any remaining flour. Chill for a further 30 minutes.

4 Meanwhile, make the raita sauce. Work the yogurt in a blender or food processor with the cucumber, mint jelly and salt and pepper to taste. Pour into a jug or bowl and chill until serving time.

5 Thread the kebabs on to oiled skewers. Mix together the oil and remaining chilli powder and brush over the kebabs. Place on the oiled grid of a preheated barbecue (or grill) and cook for 5-6 minutes, turning constantly and brushing with oil. Serve hot or cold, with the sauce handed separately.

6 Serve the kebabs and sauce with hot saffron rice or a rice salad.

TARRAGON CHICKEN SALAD

Serves 4-6

1.5 kg (3 lb) chicken, with giblets

1 medium carrot, peeled and roughly chopped

1 onion, peeled and stuck with 3 cloves

2 celery sticks, roughly chopped

6 black peppercorns

2 tablespoons chopped fresh tarragon or 1 tablespoon dried tarragon

salt

600 ml (1 pint) water

6 tablespoons thick mayonnaise (see right)

1½ tablespoons lemon juice

2 tablespoons mango chutney, finely chopped

1 garlic clove, peeled and crushed

freshly ground black pepper

2 avocados

radicchio or lettuce leaves

To garnish:

fresh tarragon sprigs (if available)

Preparation time: *30 minutes, plus cooling and chilling*
Cooking time: *1 hour 5 minutes*

1 Put the chicken and separate giblets (without the liver) in a large saucepan into which the bird just fits. Add the vegetables, peppercorns, half the tarragon and 1 teaspoon salt, then pour in the water. Bring to the boil, then cover and simmer for 1 hour or until the chicken is tender. Remove the pan from the heat and leave the chicken in the liquid until just cool.

2 Remove the chicken and take the meat off the bones. Discard all skin and cut into neat, even-sized pieces.

3 Put the mayonnaise in a large bowl with 4 tablespoons of the chicken liquid, 1 tablespoon of the lemon juice, the mango chutney, garlic, remaining tarragon, and salt and pepper to taste. Beat well, then fold in the chicken. Chill for 30 minutes.

To make your own delicious mayonnaise, you need 150 ml (¼ pint) oil for each egg yolk. The kind of oil you use is a matter of personal taste; sunflower oil is light in both flavour and colour, olive oil is stronger, so try a combination of the two. Beat the egg yolk and ½ teaspoon mustard powder in a bowl with a balloon whisk or electric beater. Add salt and pepper to taste, then beat in the oil a drop at a time until the egg and oil emulsify and become thick. Continue adding oil in a thin, steady stream, then beat in lemon juice or wine vinegar according to both taste and until the required consistency.

Seekh Kebabs; Tarragon Chicken Salad; Stuffed Courgettes

4 Peel and stone the avocados, then slice the flesh neatly. Add three-quarters of the avocado slices to the chicken and fold mixture gently in.

5 Arrange the radicchio or lettuce leaves in the bottom of a serving bowl. Sprinkle with salt and pepper, then place the chicken salad in the centre. Garnish with tarragon the remaining avocado slices, sprinkle immediately with the remaining lemon juice.

6 Serve with fresh French bread or crisp rolls and butter, and a chilled dry white wine.

STUFFED COURGETTES

100 g (4 oz) burghul (see right)
8 large courgettes
salt
2 tablespoons olive oil
1 onion, peeled and chopped
1 celery stick, finely chopped
1 garlic clove, peeled and crushed
50 g (2 oz) pine nuts, roughly chopped
2 teaspoons chopped fresh thyme
4 teaspoons chopped fresh mint
freshly ground black pepper
50 g (2 oz) butter
450 ml (¾ pint) dry white wine and water, mixed
2 tablespoons flour
4 tablespoons single cream

Preparation time: 20 minutes
Cooking time: about 45 minutes
Oven: 180°C, 350°F, Gas Mark 4

1 Put the burghul in a heatproof bowl, pour over enough boiling water just to cover, then leave for 10 minutes.

2 Meanwhile, cut the courgettes in half lengthways and scoop out the seeds and some of the flesh from the centres. Blanch the courgette shells in boiling salted water for 4 minutes, then drain and pat dry with paper towels.

3 Heat the oil in a heavy-based saucepan, add the onion, celery and garlic and fry gently until soft. Squeeze the burghul in a clean teatowel to remove excess moisture, then add to the pan with the pine nuts; toss gently. Remove from the heat and stir in half the herbs, and salt and pepper.

4 Stuff the courgette shells with the burghul mixture and sandwich them together in pairs. Place them close together in a well-buttered baking dish, dot with 25 g (1 oz) butter and pour over half the wine and water. Sprinkle with salt and pepper to taste. Cover with buttered foil. Place in a preheated oven and cook for 30 minutes.

5 Melt the remaining butter in a heavy-based saucepan, sprinkle in the flour and cook, stirring, for 1-2 minutes. Beat in the remaining wine and water a little at a time and simmer, stirring constantly. Strain and add the cooking liquid from the courgettes. Simmer until thickened, stirring constantly, then whisk in the cream over very low heat. Add the remaining herbs with salt and pepper to taste. Serve the courgettes with a little of the sauce poured over.

Burghul, sometimes also called burgul or bulgur, is available at health food shops. It is precooked cracked wheat, which usually needs soaking – either in cold water for 30 minutes, or in boiling water for 10 minutes. In Middle Eastern cookery it is highly valued for its nutty flavour and high nutritional content – it is rich in protein, minerals and B vitamins.

Open sandwiches, called smørrebrod in Denmark, are an essential part of the national cuisine. Whether a simple sandwich for a packed lunch or an elaborate display for a special occasion, the Danes attach great importance to presentation and garnish. Make sure you spread the bread for the base generously with butter; the Danes call this 'tooth butter', because you can see the pattern of your teeth in the butter when you bite into the sandwich.

DANISH OPEN CRAB SANDWICHES

4 thin slices white bread, from a large loaf

75 g (3 oz) unsalted butter, softened

crisp lettuce leaves

salt

freshly ground black pepper

8 cooked asparagus spears, fresh or canned

150 ml (¼ pint) thick mayonnaise (page 40)

2 hard-boiled egg yolks, finely chopped or sieved

1 teaspoon wine vinegar

1 tablespoon chopped fresh herbs (e.g. tarragon, chives or parsley)

2 tablespoons whipped cream

225 g (8 oz) white crabmeat (see right)

To garnish:

slices lemon

sprigs of parsley

Preparation time: 40 minutes

1 Spread the bread right to the edges with the butter, then halve each slice. Place 2 slices on each serving plate. Place lettuce leaves on top. Sprinkle with salt and pepper and set aside.

2 Chop the asparagus, reserving 8 whole tips for the garnish. Stir the chopped asparagus into the mayonnaise with the hard-boiled egg yolks, the wine vinegar and herbs.

3 Fold the whipped cream into the mayonnaise mixture, then the flaked white crabmeat. Taste and adjust the seasoning. **A** Divide the mixture equally between the lettuce leaves and garnish with the lemon slices, parsley sprigs and the reserved asparagus tips. **A**

4 Serve the sandwiches in the Danish tradition with glasses of ice-cold lager. **A** The sandwiches can be made up to 2 hours in advance. Place them on a large platter and cover loosely with a clean tea towel to help keep them fresh.

Alternatively, make the crab and asparagus mayonnaise topping up to 4 hours in advance.

1 *Twist the 8 crab legs until they snap off. Twist the 2 claws away from the direction of the pincers and pull off. Set aside. Stand the crab upright. Separate the body from the shell by pushing it away with your thumbs.*

2 *Discard the body's feathery greyish gills (dead men's fingers). Halve the body and dig out all the white flesh with a skewer or trussing needle into a bowl.*

3 *Crack the claws and legs with a sharp knock using a small hammer, rolling pin or nutcrackers and extract the white flesh with your fingers and a skewer or trussing needle. Discard any cartilage. Add the white flesh to the bowl.*

4 *Discard the stomach sac (from between the eyes) and any green matter from the shell. With a teaspoon, scoop out all the soft dark meat from the shell and place in a separate bowl.*

LA PARMIGIANA

Serves 4-6

2 large aubergines

salt

about 150 ml (¼ pint) olive oil

1 onion, peeled and roughly chopped

1 large garlic clove, peeled and crushed

450 g (1 lb) tomatoes, roughly chopped

1 tablespoon tomato purée

2 tablespoons red or white wine, or wine vinegar

2 teaspoons chopped fresh basil or 1 teaspoon dried basil

pinch of sugar

freshly ground black pepper

2 × 120 g (4 oz) Italian Mozzarella cheese, sliced

50 g (2 oz) Parmesan cheese, grated

*Preparation time: 30 minutes,
plus dégorge of aubergines
Cooking time: 1 hour 10 minutes
Oven: 200°C, 400°F, Gas Mark 6*

1 Slice the aubergines thinly, then place in a colander, sprinkling each layer lightly with salt. Place a plate on top, weight down, then leave to dégorge for 30 minutes.

2 Heat 2 tablespoons of the oil in a heavy-based saucepan. Add the onion and garlic and fry gently until soft. Add the tomatoes and tomato purée and fry gently for a few minutes until the juices flow from the tomatoes, stirring constantly to help break them up. Add the wine or vinegar, the basil, sugar and salt and pepper to taste and stir well to mix. Simmer, covered, for 20 minutes, stirring occasionally. **A**

3 Meanwhile, rinse the aubergine slices under cold running water, then pat dry with paper towels. Heat about 4 tablespoons of the remaining oil in a frying pan until very hot. Add enough aubergine slices to cover the base of the pan in a single layer and fry for about 3 minutes on each side until golden. Remove with a fish slice and drain on paper towels. Repeat with the remaining aubergine slices in batches, adding and heating more oil as necessary.

4 Liquidize the tomato sauce in an electric blender or food processor, then sieve to remove skin and seeds. Pour a thin layer of tomato sauce over the base of an ovenproof serving dish. Cover with a layer of aubergine slices, then with a layer of Mozzarella cheese and a sprinkling of Parmesan. Repeat these layers until all the ingredients are used, finishing with a fairly thick layer of Parmesan. **A** **F** Place in a preheated oven and cook for 40 minutes until golden brown and bubbling.

5 Serve la parmigiana hot or warm with a green salad.

A The tomato sauce can be made up to 3 days in advance chilled.
Alternatively, make the dish up to the baking stage up to 24 hours in advance and chill.

F Open freeze in the dish, then turn out and wrap in foil. Freeze for up to 1 month. To serve, unwrap and return to the dish. Bake from frozen, allowing 15 minutes extra cooking time and covering with foil if the topping becomes too brown.

*Danish Open Crab
Sandwiches; La
Parmigiana*

La parmigiana is an immensely popular summertime dish in Italy, when aubergines and tomatoes are so plentiful. It is also delicious served cold, cut into portions and eaten with the fingers.
Do not try to save time on preparation by cutting out the salting of the aubergines. This process, known as 'dégorger' in French, is a very important one, because the salt draws out the bitter juice from the aubergine flesh. Always leave the salt on the aubergines for the time stated, then rinse and dry thoroughly.

WINTER LUNCHES

*I*n wintertime, all thoughts of salads and slimming seem to fly out of the window. We usually crave for hot, filling lunches: it helps take our minds off the weather!

Don't choose the wintertime to cut down on portion sizes and introduce new foods, especially if these are the low-calorie type! Get back to basics, give your family and friends what they really want – traditional foods which are always best to ward off the effects of bad weather. You have the rest of the year to experiment with new ideas.

Winter is the time when you might also like to make puddings at lunchtime – somehow fresh fruit and cheese or yogurt do not have quite the same appeal in winter as they do in summer.

In this section there's a choice of traditional wintertime dishes from all over the world. There are soups from Austria, America and Scotland, a lamb dish from France, a risotto from Italy, plus chicken from Britain and a mouthwatering potato idea from the U.S.A.

Goulash soup is an Austrian recipe – called gulaschsuppe *in Austria. It is a popular lunchtime dish in the Austrian Tyrol, when skiers in wintertime stop for something warming and filling. Beer is the traditional drink to have with* gulaschsuppe, *or* glühwein, *a hot red wine spiced with cinnamon and cloves.*

GOULASH SOUP

Serves 6

50 g (2 oz) beef dripping or lard

2 large onions, peeled and thinly sliced

1 garlic clove, peeled and crushed

450 g (1 lb) chuck steak or shin of beef, trimmed of fat and cut into small dice

2 teaspoons paprika

½ teaspoon dried marjoram

¼ teaspoon caraway seeds

2 tablespoons tomato purée

1.2 litres (2 pints) beef stock

salt

freshly ground black pepper

150 ml (¼ pint) soured cream, to serve

Dumplings:

300 g (11 oz) white bread

50 g (2 oz) plain flour

¼ teaspoon dried marjoram

¼ teaspoon caraway seeds

1 egg, beaten

150 ml (¼ pint) water

Preparation time: 15 minutes
Cooking time: about 2 hours

1 Melt the dripping or lard in a large, heavy-based saucepan or flameproof casserole. Add the onions and garlic and fry gently for about 10 minutes until very soft, stirring frequently.

2 Add the beef and paprika, increase the heat and fry until well browned. Add the marjoram, caraway seeds and tomato purée and stir well to mix with the meat. Pour in the stock, bring slowly to boiling point, stirring, then add salt and pepper to taste. Cover and cook over a low heat for 1½ hours or until the meat is tender. **A** **F**

3 About 30 minutes before the end of the cooking time, make the dumplings. Cut the crusts off the bread. Break the bread into small pieces and place in a bowl. Add the flour, marjoram and caraway seeds and egg and work with a wooden spoon. Beat in the water a little at a time to make a soft, sticky dough. With well-floured hands, form into 18 balls and place on a floured board.

4 Drop the dumplings into a large pan of boiling salted water. Simmer for 15 minutes, then remove with a slotted spoon and place on top of the soup for the last 5 minutes of the cooking time. Serve hot drizzled with soured cream.

A The soup (without the dumplings) can be prepared up to 48 hours in advance. Cool, then chill. When ready to serve, reheat until bubbling while cooking the dumplings.

F Cool the soup, then pour into a rigid container, leaving headspace. Store in the freezer for up to 3 months. Thaw at room temperature for about 4 hours before reheating and cooking the dumplings.

MEDITERRANEAN LAMB CHOPS

4 'butterfly' lamb chops (see right)

2 tablespoons vegetable oil

1 small onion, peeled and finely chopped

1 garlic clove, peeled and crushed

8 canned anchovy fillets, soaked in milk for 20 minutes

2 whole red pimentos, from a 185 g (6½ oz) can, cut into thin strips

1 teaspoon dried basil or oregano

freshly ground black pepper

200 ml (7 fl oz) dry white wine

1 tablespoon tomato purée

To garnish:

sprig of fresh parsley

Preparation time: 15 minutes
Cooking time: about 30 minutes

1 Trim as much fat as possible from the chops. Heat oil in a large lidded frying pan (or 2 pans if the chops are too large to fit in 1 layer). Add the chops and fry over a moderate heat until browned on both sides. Remove and set aside.

2 Add the onion and garlic to the pan and fry gently until soft. Meanwhile, drain the anchovies, rinse under cold running water, then pat dry with paper towels. Add to the pan and fry until broken up and well mixed with the onion and garlic. Stir in the pimento.

3 Return the chops to the pan and spoon the pimento and anchovy mixture on top of each one. Sprinkle with the basil or oregano and pepper to taste. Pour the wine around the chops, stir in the tomato purée, then cover the pan with a lid. **A** Simmer for 20 minutes or until the meat is tender. Transfer to a warmed dish and garnish with parsley.

A The dish can be prepared up to 24 hours in advance up to this stage. Store in the refrigerator, then bring to boiling point before continuing with the recipe.

'Butterfly' lamb chops are cut from the loin and are also sometimes called 'double loin chops' by the butcher. Loin chops are usually sold singly, that is they are split at the backbone, but these double chops, with the backbone left in, provide a more substantial meal.

Mediterranean Lamb Chops; Goulash Soup

Chowders originated in America, where the most famous of them all is New England clam chowder. There are many different versions of chowder, but the consistency is always thick and the ingredients substantial – chowders are main meal soups rather than first courses. Fish is one of the most popular ingredients in chowder, but to ring the changes you can use chunks of ham or chicken instead of the tuna here.

CHUNKY TUNA CHOWDER

Serves 4-6

25 g (1 oz) butter or margarine

2 tablespoons vegetable oil

1 large onion, peeled and finely chopped

2 celery sticks, trimmed and finely chopped

1 green pepper, cored, seeded and diced

2 medium potatoes, peeled and diced

1.2 litres (2 pints) water

1 bay leaf

a few parsley sprigs

salt

freshly ground black pepper

2 tablespoons plain flour

300 ml (½ pint) milk

1 × 350 g (12 oz) can sweetcorn, drained

1 × 200 g (7 oz) can tuna in brine, drained

paprika

Preparation time: 20 minutes
Cooking time: about 45 minutes

1 Melt the butter or margarine with the oil in a large saucepan. Add the onion, celery and green pepper and fry gently, stirring, for 5 minutes until softened. Add the potatoes and fry for a further few minutes.

2 Pour in the water and add the herbs and salt and pepper to taste. Bring to the boil, then lower the heat, cover and simmer for 20 minutes or until the potatoes are tender but not broken up. **A**

3 In a jug, mix the flour to a paste with a little of the milk, then stir in the remaining milk. Discard the bay leaf and parsley sprigs from the cooking liquid. Pour in the milk, stirring all the time. Bring to the boil and simmer until slightly thickened. **A**

4 Add the sweetcorn and tuna to the pan and heat through for about 5 minutes. Taste and adjust the seasoning, then pour into a warmed soup tureen or individual bowls. Sprinkle with paprika and serve immediately, while piping hot. This chowder needs no accompaniment.

A Make the soup the day before either up to the first or final stage, whichever is most convenient. Cool and store in the refrigerator until ready to continue with the recipe.

CHICKEN IN A BRICK

1½ kg (3½ lb) oven-ready chicken, giblets removed

100 g (4 oz) unsalted butter, plus a little extra, softened

grated rind of 1 orange

grated rind of 1 lemon (reserve the remaining lemon)

4 tablespoons orange juice

2 garlic cloves, peeled and crushed

salt

freshly ground black pepper

150 ml (¼ pint) chicken stock

4 tablespoons dry sherry

To garnish:

orange and lemon slices

sprigs of fresh parsley

Preparation time: about 30 minutes, plus soaking time for brick
Cooking time: 1 hour 40 minutes
Oven: 230°C, 450°F, Gas Mark 8

1 Soak the chicken brick in cold water for 10-30 minutes (see right).

2 Meanwhile, wash the chicken inside and out, then pat dry with paper towels.

3 Put the butter in a bowl. Sprinkle in the orange and lemon rind, then add 2 tablespoons orange juice, the garlic and salt and pepper to taste. Beat with a wooden spoon until evenly mixed.

4 With your fingers, carefully lift the skin away from the breast of the chicken. Ease your fingers between the skin and the flesh until they are separated over the whole breast. Spread about two-thirds of the citrus butter over the flesh under the skin.

5 Prick the derinded lemon all over with a fine skewer, then place inside the body cavity of the chicken. Truss with string. **A**

6 Remove the chicken brick from the water. Place the chicken in the brick and spread the remaining butter over the skin, particularly on the legs. Sprinkle liberally with salt and pepper. Put the cover on the chicken brick and place in a cold oven. Turn the oven on and cook for 1½ hours, without opening the oven door.

7 Remove the brick from the oven, uncover and pour off the cooking juices into a saucepan. Return the chicken to the oven, and turn the oven off. Cook, uncovered, for a further 10 minutes to crisp the skin.

Chicken bricks are available at kitchen specialist shops. They are a wonderful way of cooking chicken as they give a 'roast' finish with a moist flesh, which is far more succulent than by dry roasting. When you buy a chicken brick, check the manufacturer's instructions before soaking it. Most bricks should be soaked in cold water for 30 minutes before using them for the first time, then 10 minutes for each subsequent time.

8 Meanwhile, add the stock and sherry to the juices in the pan, with the remaining orange juice. Bring to the boil and simmer for a few minutes, stirring. Taste and adjust the seasoning.

9 Transfer the chicken to a warmed serving platter, remove the trussing string and garnish with orange and lemon slices and parsley. Serve hot, with the sauce handed separately.

10 Serve with rice and seasonal vegetables.

A The chicken can be prepared up to the cooking stage 1-2 hours in advance, if convenient. Chill in the refrigerator; bring to room temperature for about 30 minutes before cooking, while soaking the brick.

Chunky Tuna Chowder; Chicken in a Brick

Cock-a-leekie Soup;
Crunchy Potato
Skins

COCK-A-LEEKIE SOUP

2 chicken portions, each weighing
about 275 g (10 oz)

4 leeks, trimmed, sliced and washed

few sprigs of thyme and parsley

salt

freshly ground black pepper

1.5 litres (2½ pints) water

8 'no-need-to-soak' prunes, stoned
(if necessary) and halved

4 tablespoons long grain rice

To garnish:

chopped fresh parsley

Preparation time: *20 minutes,*
plus cooling
Cooking time: *about 1 hour*

1 Put the chicken portions in a large saucepan. Add the leeks, herbs, 1 teaspoon salt and pepper to taste. Pour in the water and bring slowly to the boil. Lower the heat, half cover with a lid and

simmer gently for 30 minutes or until the chicken is tender. **A F M**

2 Remove the chicken from the liquid and leave until cool enough to handle.

3 Meanwhile, discard the sprigs of herbs from the cooking liquid, then add the prunes and rice and bring back to the boil. Simmer again for 10 minutes.

4 Take the flesh off the chicken bones and cut into bite-sized pieces, discarding the skin. Add to the pan and continue simmering for 10 minutes or until the rice and chicken are really tender. **A F M** Taste and adjust seasoning, then pour into a warmed soup tureen or individual bowls. Sprinkle with chopped parsley and serve piping hot.

A The soup can be made 24 hours in advance up to the end of step 1. Leave until cold, then chill. When ready to serve, remove any solidified fat from the surface of the soup, then reheat and continue with the recipe.

Alternatively, make the soup com

To be absolutely correct, cock-a-leekie from Scotland should be made with a whole boiling fowl. The broth and vegetables should be eaten as a first course, then the meat cut up and served as a main course. This version, using chicken portions, is more suitable for lunchtime. To make it even quicker, use skinned boneless chunks of chicken, available fresh and frozen at supermarkets.

Use the leftover cooked potato from this recipe for bubble and squeak with cheese (page 16).

pletely the day before and simply reheat until bubbling when required.

F Cool, then turn into a rigid container, leaving headspace. Freeze for up to 3 months. Thaw from frozen on top of the cooker, then continue with the recipe or serve, depending on stage at which the soup was frozen.

M To thaw, turn into a suitable dish. Cook on defrost power for 15-20 minutes. Break up with a fork when possible. Complete as above, depending on stage reached.

CRUNCHY POTATO SKINS

Serves 2

2 large baking potatoes

4 rashers middle bacon

100 g (4 oz) Cheddar cheese, grated

vegetable oil, for brushing

salt

freshly ground black pepper

Soured Cream Dip:

150 ml (¼ pint) soured cream

7.5 cm (3 inch) piece cucumber, finely chopped

2 tablespoons snipped chives

Preparation time: 20 minutes, plus cooling
Cooking time: about 1 hour 20 minutes
Oven: 200°C, 400°F, Gas Mark 6;

1 Scrub the potatoes clean under running water, then pat dry with paper towels. Pierce holes in the potatoes with a fine skewer, then place in a preheated oven and cook for 1¼ hours or until tender.

2 Meanwhile, make the dip. Mix together the soured cream, cucumber and chives with salt and pepper to taste. Pour into a serving bowl and chill in the refrigerator until serving time.

3 Grill the bacon until crisp. Leave until cool enough to handle, then snip into small pieces with kitchen scissors, cutting off and discarding the rinds. Mix the cheese with the bacon pieces.

4 When the potatoes are soft, remove from the oven and cut in half lengthways. Leave until cool enough to handle, then scoop out the flesh with a teaspoon, leaving a thin layer of flesh next to the skin. Cut each potato skin in half lengthways again, to make 4 quarters for each serving.

5 Brush the potatoes inside and out with a little oil, then sprinkle the insides with salt and pepper to taste. Divide the cheese and bacon mixture evenly between the potato skins, then place on a baking sheet and return to the oven for 5 minutes until the cheese is melted.

6 Serve hot, with the soured cream dip handed separately.

RISI E BISI

25 g (1 oz) butter

2 tablespoons olive oil

1 small onion, peeled and finely chopped

1 garlic clove, peeled and crushed

350 g (12 oz) Italian risotto rice (see right)

4 tablespoons dry white wine

900 ml-1.2 litres (1½-2 pints) hot chicken stock

225 g (8 oz) frozen peas

225 g (8 oz) boiled ham, diced

salt

freshly ground black pepper

To serve:

freshly grated Parmesan cheese

Preparation time: 10 minutes
Cooking time: about 25 minutes

1 Melt the butter with the oil in a large, heavy-based saucepan. Add the onion and garlic and fry gently until soft. Add the rice and stir to coat in the onion mixture, then add the wine. Cook gently, stirring, until the rice has absorbed the wine.

2 Add 300 ml (½ pint) of the stock and continue cooking gently until absorbed, stirring frequently. Add a further 300 ml (½ pint) of the stock and the peas and continue cooking and stirring – the rice should become tender and creamy as it absorbs the liquid.

3 Add the ham and salt and pepper to taste, and a few tablespoons of stock. Continue cooking and stirring until the rice and peas are quite tender, adding stock by the tablespoonful as necessary – the finished dish should be moist and creamy and the amount of stock needed will vary

4 Serve hot in individual bowls, with grated Parmesan to sprinkle liberally over the top. Dry white wine and a green salad make good accompaniments.

The Italian risotto rice needed for risi e bisi is now available in most supermarkets. It is a medium grain rice which gives risottos their special creamy quality – the liquid is added and absorbed gradually, unlike other methods in which the water and rice are cooked together from the beginning. The best types of Italian risotto rice to buy are called arborio and avorio, but you will only be able to ask for these by name in specialist Italian shops. Most Italians would describe risi e bisi as a cross between a soup and a risotto, and it is often eaten with a spoon and fork.

WHOLEFOOD LUNCHES

D on't be misled by the term 'wholefood' into thinking this is a section of cranky foods. Nowadays the accent is on nutritious ingredients which are as natural as they can be – without the addition of preservatives, additives and artificial colourings.

Tandoori Burgers;
Tabbouleh Casserole

It isn't even necessary to make a special trip to a health food shop to buy wholefood these days. Most supermarkets have a good choice of natural ingredients – 100% and 85% wholewheat flours, unbleached white flour, pulses, wholewheat and spinach pasta, raw brown and muscovado sugars, vegetable margarines, dried fruits, nuts and seeds, low-fat cheeses and yogurts, and skimmed milk, are just a few.

The recipes here should convince you that wholefood cookery is just as good and delicious as any other style of cooking. In fact you will probably enjoy eating wholefood ingredients so much that you will be converted to using them more and more often in your daily cooking, cutting out many processed foods. There is no need to go to extremes, the accent is simply on healthy eating and nutritious ingredients – lots of fresh fruit and vegetables combined with natural flours, grains, cereals, sugars, and such. You will find flavours more accentuated, and the amount of extra fibre beneficial.

Do not try to skimp on the soaking time of the yellow split peas for the tandoori lentil burgers. The peas are not boiled and therefore need this long soaking to absorb most of the water and swell. If you find it difficult to work the drained peas in your blender, add about 1 tablespoon of the soaking water and this may make it easier. Be careful not to add too much water or the burgers will not stick together. Tandoori mixture is available from Indian specialist shops, and delicatessens and supermarkets. It is a ready-mixed powder of several different spices, which gives an instant tandoori flavour to food.

TANDOORI BURGERS

Serves 4-6

450 g (1 lb) yellow split peas, soaked in cold water for 24 hours

2 tablespoons tandoori mixture (see left)

2 garlic cloves, peeled and crushed

salt

freshly ground black pepper

4 tablespoons plain wholewheat flour

2 teaspoons paprika

2 teaspoons turmeric

4 tablespoons vegetable oil

Curry Sauce:

2 tablespoons vegetable oil

2 tablespoons butter

1 onion, peeled and finely chopped

2 garlic cloves, peeled and crushed

2 teaspoons garam masala (page 31)

1 teaspoon turmeric

½ teaspoon chilli powder, or to taste

450 ml (¾ pint) vegetable stock or water

To garnish:

fresh coriander

Preparation time: *about 45 minutes, plus 24 hours soaking and chilling*
Cooking time: *about 40 minutes*

1 Drain the split peas, then place in batches in a blender and work until finely ground. Transfer to a bowl, add the tandoori mixture, garlic and salt and pepper to taste. Mix well with your hands to bind the mixture together. Form into 24 flat burger shapes, then chill for at least 30 minutes.

2 Meanwhile, make the curry sauce. Heat the oil with the butter in a flameproof casserole or large saucepan. Add the onion and garlic and fry gently until soft. Stir in the spices and fry for a few minutes more, then pour in the stock or water and bring to the boil. Add 1 teaspoon salt and simmer for at least 20 minutes, stirring occasionally.

3 Mix the flour with the paprika and turmeric on a flat plate. Use to coat the lentil burgers. Heat the oil in a frying pan until very hot. Add the burgers in batches and fry for 2 minutes on each side until browned. Remove with a slotted spoon and place in the curry sauce. **A** Simmer for 10 minutes before serving, garnished with the coriander.

4 These burgers make a nutritious meal on their own, but they can be served with brown long grain rice.

A These burgers actually improve by being made 1 day in advance. Store the burgers in the curry sauce in the refrigerator after cooling – the flavour will improve enormously for the keeping, as it does with all curried dishes.

TABBOULEH CASSEROLE

Serves 4-6

3 tablespoons vegetable oil

1 large onion, peeled and chopped

1-2 garlic cloves, peeled and crushed

4 celery sticks, sliced

about 450 g (1 lb) leeks, trimmed, sliced and washed

100 g (4 oz) mixed shelled nuts, roughly chopped

1 × 400 g (14 oz) can tomatoes

1 teaspoon yeast extract

a few drops of Tabasco sauce, to taste

900 ml (1½ pints) vegetable stock or water

3 tablespoons chopped fresh parsley

salt

freshly ground black pepper

175 g (6 oz) burghul (see right)

Preparation time: *15 minutes*
Cooking time: *35-40 minutes*

1 Heat the oil in a large flameproof casserole or heavy-based saucepan. Add the onion and garlic and fry gently until soft. Add the celery and leeks, cover and fry for 10 minutes, stirring frequently.

2 Add the nuts to the pan together with the tomatoes and their juice, the yeast extract, Tabasco and stock or water. Bring to the boil, stirring, then lower the heat, add 1 tablespoon of the parsley, and salt and pepper to taste. Simmer for 15 minutes. **A**

3 Add the burghul to the pan. Simmer, stirring constantly, for 3-5 minutes until the burghul swells and absorbs the liquid (see right). Taste and adjust the seasoning before serving sprinkled with the remaining parsley.

4 Serve with wholewheat bread rolls and margarine or butter. Or spoon into individual bowls, sprinkle with mixed grated cheese and parsley and pop under a preheated grill until golden and melted.

A The sauce can be made up to this stage up to 24 hours in advance. Cool, then store in the refrigerator.

Tabbouleh casserole is named after the Middle Eastern salad, tabbouleh, which is made of burghul (page 41), tomatoes, parsley and garlic. Take care when cooking burghul as it absorbs water very quickly. Stir it constantly as it may stick to the bottom of the pan.

You can use any dried beans you like to make bean and avocado salad. Consider the colours first and try to choose at least two or three different ones so that the finished dish looks most attractive. Red kidney beans, white haricot or black-eye beans and green flageolets would make an interesting combination, and they all cook in roughly the same amount of time. (Red kidney beans must be boiled briskly for 10 minutes.) If you boil all three beans together, the colours tend to merge so instead, boil them in separate pans.

BEAN AND AVOCADO SALAD

Serves 4-6

225 g (8 oz) mixed dried beans (see left), soaked in cold water overnight
9 tablespoons olive oil
finely grated rind of 1½ lemons
4 tablespoons lemon juice
2 teaspoons French mustard
salt
freshly ground black pepper
1 small onion, peeled and finely chopped
1 garlic clove, peeled and crushed
2 tablespoons chopped fresh mint or basil
1 ripe avocado

Preparation time: *30 minutes, plus overnight soaking*
Cooking time: *1-1½ hours, plus cooling*

1 Drain the beans, rinse under cold running water, then place in a pan (see left) and cover with fresh cold water. Bring to the boil, skim off any scum with a slotted spoon, then cover and simmer for 1-1½ hours until tender. If using red kidney beans these must be boiled briskly for 10 minutes.

2 Drain the beans thoroughly, then place in a bowl. Whisk together the olive oil, lemon rind and juice, mustard and salt and pepper to taste. Pour over the hot beans and toss gently to mix. Leave until cold, turning the beans in the dressing from time to time. **A**

3 Stir the onion, garlic and mint or basil into the salad, taste and adjust the seasoning. Halve, stone and peel the avocado, then cut the flesh into neat slices. Add to the salad and fold gently to mix. Serve immediately, before the avocado discolours.

4 For a nutritious lunch, serve with wholewheat and granary bread, and wedges of cheese.

A The salad can be prepared up to this stage up to 24 hours in advance. Cover with cling film and chill in the refrigerator until required. Bring to room temperature for 30 minutes before continuing with the recipe.

Bean and Avocado Salad; Spicy Vegetable Pie

SPICY VEGETABLE PIE

Serves 4-6

225 g (8 oz) carrots, peeled and thinly sliced
225 g (8 oz) swede or turnip, peeled and thinly sliced
225 g (8 oz) cauliflower florets
600 ml (1 pint) vegetable stock or water
100 g (4 oz) frozen peas
25 g (1 oz) vegetable margarine
100 g (4 oz) button mushrooms, sliced
3 tablespoons plain wholewheat flour
100 g (4 oz) mature Cheddar cheese, grated
2 tablespoons chopped fresh coriander or parsley
¼ teaspoon ground mace or grated nutmeg
salt
freshly ground black pepper
a little milk, to glaze
Pastry: (see far right)
75 g (3 oz) plain wholewheat flour
75 g (3 oz) plain white (unbleached) flour
pinch of salt
75 g (3 oz) vegetable margarine
25 g (1 oz) mature Cheddar cheese, grated
about 2 tablespoons cold water,

Preparation time: *30 minutes*
Cooking time: *50 minutes*
Oven: *190°C, 375°F, Gas Mark 5*

1 Make the pastry. Sift the flours and salt into a bowl, adding any bran left in the sieve. Add the margarine in small pieces and rub in with the fingertips. Stir in the cheese, then add enough cold water to mix to a dough. Gather into a ball with one hand, wrap in cling film or foil and leave to rest in a cold place or chill while making the filling. **A**

2 Put the carrots, swede or turnip and cauliflower in a heavy-based saucepan and pour in the stock or water. Bring to the boil, cover and simmer for 5-7 minutes, until just barely tender. Add the frozen peas for the last 2 minutes.

3 With a slotted spoon, transfer the vegetables to a 1.2 litre (2 pint) pie dish. Pour the cooking liquid into a measuring jug.

4 Melt the margarine in the pan, add the mushrooms and fry gently for 2 minutes. Transfer the mushrooms with a slotted spoon to the pie dish and mix with the other vegetables.

5 Sprinkle the flour into the juices in the pan and cook, stirring, for 1-2 minutes. Add 450 ml (¾ pint) of the vegetable cooking liquid, beating it in a little at a time. Simmer, stirring, until thick and smooth. Stir in the cheese, coriander or parsley, mace or nutmeg and salt and pepper to taste, then simmer for a further few minutes until the cheese has melted. Pour over the vegetables in the dish. **A**

6 Roll out the dough on a lightly floured surface and cut out a lid to fit the pie dish. Brush the rim of the dish with water, then place the lid on top, pressing the edge well to seal. Flute the edge, make a hole in the centre and brush the dough with a little milk to glaze. Decorate with pastry trimmings, if wished. **A** **F** Glaze the decoration. Cook in a preheated oven for 30 minutes until the pastry is golden.

7 This vegetable pie is a meal in itself, and needs no accompaniment.

A The pastry and/or filling can be made the night before. Keep chilled.
Alternatively, the pie can be made up to the cooking stage the night before. Keep in a cold place until required. Glaze just before baking.

F Open freeze until solid, then pack in a polythene bag. Store in the freezer for up to 3 months. Cook from frozen, allowing at least 15 minutes extra time. Glaze about halfway through baking. Cover with foil if the pastry overbrowns.

It is possible to make shortcrust pastry with 100% wholewheat flour, but the result does tend to be on the hard side, especially if you are unused to handling this type of pastry. Better results can be obtained by using half 85% wholewheat flour and half plain white flour. Look for unbleached white flour in supermarkets and health food shops; it does not have the chemical additives of ordinary flour.

BUCKWHEAT PANCAKES

Makes 6

50 g (2 oz) plain white
(unbleached) flour

salt

50 g (2 oz) buckwheat flour (see left)

1 egg, beaten

300 ml (½ pint) milk

vegetable oil, for frying

Ratatouille filling:

1 small aubergine, weighing
about 150 g (5 oz)

2 tablespoons olive oil

1 small onion, peeled and finely sliced

2 garlic cloves, peeled and crushed

1 red pepper, cored, seeded
and finely sliced

225 g (8 oz) ripe tomatoes,
skinned and chopped

2 small courgettes, finely sliced

1 tablespoon tomato purée

2 teaspoons chopped fresh basil
or 1 teaspoon dried basil

freshly ground black pepper

a few tablespoons white wine
or water, to moisten if required

*Preparation time: about 25 minutes,
plus time to dégorge and standing time*
Cooking time: *about 50 minutes*

Buckwheat flour, available at health food shops, is simply buckwheat which has been very finely ground. It is an unappetizing grey colour, with dark specks of buckwheat in it, but when used in batters it makes interesting-looking pancakes. The French are very fond of using buckwheat flour to make crêpes; if you visit a crêperie, either in this country or in France, it is most likely that the crêpes will have been made with buckwheat.

1 First dégorge the aubergine for the ratatouille filling. Slice the aubergine thinly, then place in a colander, sprinkling each layer lightly with salt. Place a plate on top, weight down, then leave to dégorge (page 43) for 30 minutes.

2 Meanwhile, heat the oil in a large, heavy-based saucepan. Add the onion and garlic and fry gently until soft. Add the red pepper and fry for a few minutes, add the tomatoes and courgettes and simmer until the tomatoes release their juice.

3 Rinse the aubergines under cold running water, then add to the ratatouille with the tomato purée, basil and salt and pepper to taste. Simmer for about 30 minutes while making the pancakes, stirring occasionally and adding a little wine or water if the ratatouille seems dry. **A** **F**

4 Make the pancakes. Sift the plain flour into a bowl with a pinch of salt. Stir in the buckwheat flour, then make a well in the centre. Gradually add the egg and milk. Whisk well to combine to a smooth batter. (Alternatively, liquidize all the ingredients in a blender or food processor.) Leave the batter to stand for 30 minutes. **A**

5 Pour enough oil into a pancake pan or heavy-based frying pan just to cover the base and heat until very hot. Stir the batter well. Pour one-sixth of the batter into the pan and swirl to cover the base. Cook for 1-2 minutes until the underside is set, then turn the pancake over and cook for a further 20-30 seconds on the other side.

6 Remove the pancake from the pan and place on a plate. Spoon one-sixth of the ratatouille filling in the centre. Fold opposite sides of the pancake into the centre to make a square envelope shape, then turn the shape over. Keep hot. Continue making and filling 6 pancakes. Serve at once.

A The ratatouille filling can be made up to 24 hours in advance. Keep in a covered bowl in the refrigerator. Reheat while frying the pancakes.

The pancake batter can be made up to 4 hours in advance. Keep covered in a cold place or in the refrigerator until required.

F Freeze the ratatouille in a rigid container for up to 3 months. Reheat from frozen, adding a little water to the pan to prevent sticking.

Buckwheat Pancakes; Vegetable Lasagnes

VEGETABLE LASAGNES

Serves 6

2 tablespoons olive oil

2 small green peppers, cored, seeded and finely chopped

75 g (3 oz) margarine or butter

350 g (12 oz) button mushrooms, finely sliced

2 quantities tomato sauce (page 4)

50 g (2 oz) plain white (unbleached) flour or wholewheat flour

900 ml (1½ pints) milk

50 g (2 oz) Cheddar or Wensleydale cheese, grated

50 g (2 oz) Parmesan cheese, grated

¼ teaspoon grated nutmeg

salt

freshly ground black pepper

about 450 g (1 lb) pre-cooked lasagne (see right)

Preparation time: 45 minutes
Cooking time: 1 hour 10 minutes
Oven: 190°C, 375°F, Gas Mark 5

1 Heat the olive oil in a large, heavy-based saucepan. Add the green peppers and fry for 7-10 minutes until soft. Add 25 g (1 oz) of the margarine or butter and the mushrooms and fry for about 5 minutes. Remove the peppers and mushrooms with a slotted spoon and set aside.

2 Pour the tomato sauce into the juices in the pan and bring to the boil. Simmer, uncovered, until thick and reduced by one-third. Stir in the peppers and mushrooms and set aside.

3 Melt the remaining margarine or butter in a clean pan, sprinkle in the flour and cook, stirring, for 1-2 minutes. Remove from the heat and beat in the milk a little at a time. Return to the heat and simmer, stirring, until smooth. Add the Cheddar or Wensleydale cheese, and half of the Parmesan, the nutmeg and salt and pepper to taste. Stir over a low heat until the cheese has melted.

4 Pour a layer of cheese sauce into the bottom of 6 ovenproof dishes. Put a layer of lasagne in the dishes, then pour in enough mushroom and tomato mixture to cover. Repeat these layers until all the ingredients are used, finishing with a layer of cheese sauce. **A**

5 Cook in a preheated oven for 30 minutes. Sprinkle with the remaining Parmesan and cook for 5 minutes.

A Prepare the lasagnes up to 24 hours in advance and keep in the refrigerator. Allow a little extra cooking time.

Precooked lasagne is an absolute boon to the busy cook. Available dried it can be used straight from the packet, thus cutting out all the boiling and draining that takes up so much time. It comes in sheets which vary in size according to the manufacturer; if the sheets do not fit your dishes, simply break them to size. Three different flavours are available: plain (white), spinach and wholewheat.

SPECIAL LUNCHES

*T*he secret of successful entertaining at lunchtime, whether it's a formal affair for business colleagues or a more simple meal for close family, is not to be over ambitious and to prepare as much as you can beforehand – preferably the day or night before.

The mornings go all too quickly, even if you make a special effort to start bright and early, and you can find yourself running out of time. Guests need to feel wanted and receive a calm welcome at lunchtime, just as they do for a dinner party, so it is worth preparing as much as possible in advance. Aim to complete all shopping, with the exception of last minute fresh items such as bread and salad ingredients. Even the table can be set for lunch the night before; and don't forget to leave half an hour or so before your guests arrive to change and get yourself ready.

These recipes have been carefully thought out so that the majority of the work can be done at least the day before. They are a little more complicated and time-consuming than in other sections in the book, but this is to be expected when entertaining, and you are sure to feel it has been worthwhile on the day.

For the Cumberland sauce to serve with the stuffed crown roast put 4 tablespoons redcurrant jelly in a saucepan with 150 ml (¼ pint) each red wine and stock or water, the finely grated rind of 1 orange, 3 tablespoons orange juice, ¼ teaspoon ground cinnamon and salt and pepper to taste. Heat gently, stirring, until the redcurrant jelly has melted, then simmer for about 5 minutes to allow the flavours to develop. Serve hot or cold.

STUFFED CROWN ROAST

Serves 4-6
1 crown roast of lamb with 12-16 cutlets
vegetable oil, for brushing
salt
freshly ground black pepper
Cumberland sauce (see left)
Stuffing:
25 g (1 oz) butter or margarine
1 small onion, peeled and finely chopped
2 celery sticks, finely chopped
100 g (4 oz) stoned dried apricots, finely chopped
50 g (2 oz) blanched almonds, finely chopped
100 g (4 oz) wholewheat or granary breadcrumbs
3 tablespoons chopped fresh mint
1 egg, beaten

Preparation time: 25 minutes
Cooking time: 2 hours 5 minutes
Oven: 200°C, 400°F, Gas Mark 6; then 180°C, 350°F, Gas Mark 4

1 Ask your butcher to prepare the crown roast of lamb from 2 best ends neck of lamb. (You may have to order it.)
2 Make the stuffing. Melt the butter or margarine in a small saucepan, add the onion and celery and fry gently for 5 minutes or until softened. Transfer to a bowl and add the remaining stuffing ingredients, with salt and pepper to taste. Mix well with your hands to bind the ingredients together.
3 Remove the cutlet frills from the crown roast and reserve. Cover the ends of the bones with foil to prevent them burning. Stand the crown roast in a well-oiled roasting tin. Fill the centre with the stuffing and cover with foil. **A**
4 Brush the joint liberally with oil and sprinkle all over with salt and pepper. Roast in a preheated oven for 30 minutes, then reduce the oven temperature and roast for a further 1½ hours. Remove the foil covering from the stuffing for the last 15 minutes. Transfer the joint to a warmed serving platter. Replace the foil from the bones with the reserved cutlet frills.
5 Serve with Cumberland sauce and traditional roast vegetables.
A Prepare up to roasting the night before. Keep in the refrigerator.

CANARD CASSIS

4 duck breast fillets, each weighing about 175 g (6 oz)
1 × 350 g (12 oz) jar blackcurrants in syrup
finely grated rind of 1 orange
3 tablespoons orange juice
4 tablespoons crème de cassis
freshly ground black pepper
40 g (1½ oz) butter
1 tablespoon olive oil
salt
To garnish:
blanched orange shreds

Preparation time: 20 minutes, plus marinating
Cooking time: about 15 minutes

1 Skin the duck breasts and place in a shallow dish. Drain the syrup from the blackcurrants into the dish, reserving the blackcurrants. Add the orange rind and juice to the duck with the crème de cassis and pepper to taste. Cover and marinate in the refrigerator for at least 4 hours, turning the duck breasts in the marinade from time to time. **A**
2 Remove the duck breasts from the marinade and pat dry with paper towels. Reserve the marinade. Melt 25 g (1 oz) butter with the oil in a large, heavy-based frying pan. Add the duck breasts and fry over a moderate heat for 7-8 minutes on each side or until tender. Remove the duck from the pan, sprinkle with salt and pepper and keep warm in a covered dish in the oven.
3 Pour the reserved marinade into the pan and bring to the boil, stirring to scrape up the sediment. Simmer until a syrupy sauce is formed, stirring constantly. Lower the heat, add the remaining butter and 4 tablespoons blackcurrants and heat through. Taste and adjust the seasoning.
4 To serve, slice the duck breasts diagonally across the grain. Spoon the sauce around the duck breasts, put the blackcurrants on top and sprinkle with orange shreds. Serve at once.
5 Serve with a salad of watercress and curly endive in a walnut oil dressing and gratin dauphinois potatoes (see right).
A The duck can be marinated in the refrigerator for up to 48 hours, provided really fresh when bought. Turn them in the marinade occasionally.

For gratin dauphinois to serve with canard cassis: put 1 kg (2 lb) floury potatoes (peeled and thinly sliced) in a lightly greased shallow ovenproof dish. Melt 40 g (1½ oz) butter and fry 2 garlic cloves (peeled and halved). Discard the garlic and pour the butter over the potatoes. Heat 300 ml (½ pint) milk and 120 ml (4 fl oz) single cream, add salt and pepper and a pinch of grated nutmeg. Pour over the potatoes. Cover with foil and cook in a preheated oven 180°C, 350°F, Gas Mark 4 for about 40 minutes. Remove the foil, sprinkle with 125 g (4 oz) grated Emmenthal or Gruyère cheese and cook for 20 minutes at 200°C, 400°F, Gas Mark 6.

Stuffed Crown Roast; Canard Cassis

Filo pastry is available, both fresh and frozen, at continental and Greek or Cypriot delicatessens and bakers. It is the paper thin pastry used in Greek cookery to make sticky pastries like baklava, and in Germany cookery to make apfelstrudel. Be careful when using filo pastry: once the packet is opened it tends to dry out very quickly and become brittle. Cover it with a damp teatowel while you are making the scallop and mushroom rolls.

SCALLOP AND MUSHROOM ROLLS

Makes 12 rolls

350 g (12 oz) fresh or frozen scallops
25 g (1 oz) butter
1 tablespoon olive oil
225 g (8 oz) button mushrooms, roughly chopped
150 ml (¼ pint) dry white wine
4 teaspoons chopped fresh basil or 2 teaspoons dried basil
salt
freshly ground black pepper
12 sheets filo pastry (see left), each measuring 40 × 20 cm (16 × 8 inches)
vegetable oil, for brushing
150 ml (¼ pint) single cream

Preparation time: *30 minutes*
Cooking time: *20-25 minutes*
Oven: *200°C, 400°F, Gas Mark 6*

1 Rinse the scallops under cold running water, then dry thoroughly with paper towels. Slice into small pieces.

2 Melt the butter with the oil in a heavy-based saucepan, add the mushrooms and fry gently. Remove the mushrooms with a slotted spoon and set aside.

3 Add the scallops to the pan and fry gently for 5 minutes, stirring constantly. Pour in the wine, add half the basil and salt and pepper to taste. Simmer gently for 5 minutes, then remove with a slotted spoon and mix with the mushrooms. Reserve the liquid in the pan.

4 Use one sheet of filo pastry and one-twelfth of the scallop and mushroom mixture to make 1 roll (see right).

5 Place the roll on an oiled baking sheet and seal the remaining corner of the roll with oil. Brush all over with a little more oil. Repeat with the remaining filling and sheets of pastry to make 12 rolls. **A** Cook in a preheated oven for 5-7 minutes until golden.

6 Meanwhile, make the sauce. Pour the cream into the reserved liquid in the pan and heat through, stirring constantly. Taste and adjust the seasoning.

7 Arrange 3 rolls on each of 4 warmed plates. Drizzle sauce over the rolls and sprinkle with the remaining basil.

8 Serve at once with a fennel and curly endive salad.

A The rolls can be made up to cooking the night before. Store both rolls and reserved cooking liquid in the refrigerator.

1 *Brush one half of a sheet of filo pastry with oil. Fold the plain half over to make a 20 cm (8 inch) square.*

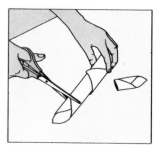

2 *Spread ¹⁄₁₂ of the scallop and mushroom mixture on the pastry square, spreading it diagonally across one corner.*

3 *Neatly roll the filo pastry up over the filling and continue rolling until the opposite corner is reached.*

4 *With kitchen scissors, cut off the ends of the roll.*

FISH TERRINE IN GINGER SAUCE

Serves 6

Terrine:

vegetable oil, for brushing

1 kg (2 lb) thick cod (in one piece)

300 ml (½ pint) dry white wine

300 ml (½ pint) water

¼ onion, peeled and sliced

2 slices of lemon

1 bay leaf

a few black peppercorns

40 g (1½ oz) butter

65 g (2½ oz) plain flour

150 ml (¼ pint) double cream

2 whole eggs

2 egg yolks

2 tablespoons chopped fresh parsley

4 teaspoons chopped fresh tarragon
or 2 teaspoons dried tarragon

¼ teaspoon grated nutmeg

salt

freshly ground black pepper

225 g (8 oz) prawns, peeled
and chopped

Sauce:

a few saffron threads

150 ml (¼ pint) dry white wine

2 tablespoons chopped stem ginger,
with syrup

4 tablespoons double cream

*Preparation time: 30 minutes,
plus standing*
Cooking time: about 2 hours
Oven: 180°C, 350°F, Gas Mark 4

1 Brush the inside of a 1.2 litre (2 pint) soufflé dish lightly with oil, line the base with greaseproof paper, then brush the paper lightly with oil. Set aside.

2 Put the cod in a large saucepan with the wine, water, onion, lemon, bay leaf and peppercorns. Simmer gently for 15 minutes or until the fish flakes when tested with a fork.

3 Remove the fish from the liquid and flake the flesh, discarding the skin and bones. Strain the cooking liquid into a measuring jug and reserve. Mince the fish finely or work in a blender or food processor. Drain off any surplus liquid and set aside.

4 Melt the butter in a clean, large saucepan, sprinkle in the flour and cook, stirring, for 1-2 minutes. Remove from the heat and beat in 450 ml (¾ pint) of the reserved cooking liquid a little at a time. Return to the heat and simmer, stirring, until very thick and smooth.

5 Remove the pan from the heat. Beat in the minced fish, cream, eggs, egg yolks, herbs, nutmeg and salt and pepper to taste.

6 Spoon half of the fish mixture into the prepared soufflé dish. Arrange a layer of prawns on top, then spoon over the remaining fish mixture. Cover the dish with oiled greaseproof paper. **A** Stand the dish in a roasting tin half filled with hot water. Cook in a preheated oven for 1½ hours or until the mixture feels firm when tested with a skewer. Remove from the water and leave to settle for 20-30 minutes.

7 Meanwhile, make the sauce. Bring the remaining fish cooking liquid to the boil in a pan with the saffron threads, then remove from the heat. Leave to stand for 10 minutes, then add the wine, ginger and cream. Simmer, stirring, until hot, adding salt and pepper.

8 Run a palette knife round the edge of the terrine and turn out on to a warmed serving plate. Peel off the lining paper. Pour a little of the sauce over the terrine and hand the remainder separately in a jug.

9 Serve with French bread and a salad.
A Make the terrine up to cooking the day before. Store in the refrigerator.

*Scallop and
Mushroom Rolls;
Fish Terrine in
Ginger Sauce*

Get your butcher to bone the loin of pork for Armenian pork. Order at least 24 hours in advance and ask him for the thickest end of the loin, if possible. Most butchers leave the skin on for the crackling, but for this recipe it needs to be cut off with most of the fat as it would spoil the appearance of the finished dish when cold. The butcher does not need to roll and tie the joint after boning because you are going to stuff it yourself.

ARMENIAN PORK

Serves 8
2.5 kg (5½ lb) loin of pork, skinned and boned (see left)
4 tablespoons redcurrant jelly
2 teaspoons dried oregano
finely grated rind of 2 oranges
salt
freshly ground black pepper
225 g (8 oz) 'no need to soak' prunes
about 40 g (1½ oz) split blanched almonds
vegetable oil, for brushing
300 ml (½ pint) full-bodied red wine
6 tablespoons orange juice
To garnish:
orange slices
sprigs of fresh parsley

Preparation time: *about 30 minutes*
Cooking time: *about 2 hours 40 minutes (depending on exact size of joint), plus cooling*
Oven: *160°C, 325°F, Gas Mark 3*

1 Weigh the boned and skinned joint and calculate the cooking time, allowing 40 minutes per 450 g (1 lb). Place the joint on a board or work surface, skinned side facing downwards. With a sharp knife, cut along the length of the meat to make a slit underneath the 'eye' of the loin.

2 Melt half the redcurrant jelly and brush along the slit in the pork, then sprinkle with the oregano, orange rind and salt and pepper to taste.

3 Stone the prunes if necessary and stuff each one with an almond. Place the prunes along the slit in the pork.

4 Roll up the meat and tie at regular intervals with string. Stand the joint in a well-oiled roasting tin. Melt the remaining redcurrant jelly and brush all over the meat together with a little vegetable oil. Sprinkle liberally with salt and pepper, then pour in the wine and orange juice.

5 Roast the joint in a preheated oven for the calculated time, turning and basting every 30 minutes. Leave the joint to cool in the cooking liquid, turning occasionally, then remove from the tin and wrap in foil. Keep in the refrigerator until ready to serve. **A**

6 Serve cold for a buffet lunch party: slice the joint neatly and arrange overlapping slices on a platter. Garnish with slices of orange and parsley.

A The cooked pork will keep for up to 3 days in the refrigerator. Allow to come to room temperature for at least 1 hour before serving.

PARTY PAVLOVA

Serves 6-8
vegetable oil, for brushing
4 egg whites
good pinch of salt
225 g (8 oz) caster sugar
1¼ teaspoons cornflour
1¼ teaspoons vinegar
1 teaspoon vanilla flavouring
Topping:
150 ml (¼ pint) double cream
150 ml (¼ pint) single cream
2 ripe peaches or nectarines, skinned, halved, stoned and neatly sliced
225 g (8 oz) strawberries, hulled and sliced
2 kiwi fruit, peeled and sliced
225 g (8 oz) seedless white grapes
4 tablespoons orange-flavoured liqueur
finely grated rind of 1 orange
3 tablespoons orange juice
2 tablespoons caster sugar, or to taste

Preparation time: *30-40 minutes*
Cooking time: *1½ hours, plus cooling*
Oven: *120°C, 250°F, Gas Mark ½*

1 Line a large baking sheet with greased greaseproof paper or non-stick silicone paper and brush lightly with oil. Set aside.

2 Put the egg whites and salt in a large bowl and beat until very stiff and standing in peaks. Add half the sugar and beat again until shiny. Mix the remaining sugar with the cornflour and fold into the meringue with a large metal spoon. Stir in the vinegar and vanilla flavouring.

3 Spoon the meringue into a large piping bag fitted with a large plain nozzle. Pipe a 25 cm (10 inch) circle on to the prepared baking sheet, starting in the centre and working outwards in a spiral. Pipe a second layer of meringue around the edge of the circle on top of the first layer, to make a raised edge.

4 Bake in a preheated oven for 1½ hours until dry and crisp. Ease the pavlova off the paper with a palette knife, then transfer to a wire tray and leave to cool. **A**

Pavlova, the Australian 'marshmallow' meringue dessert, was named after the Russian ballerina Anna Pavlova when she visited Australia on tour. It is crisp on the outside, like other meringues, but soft and gooey, like marshmallow, in the centre. It is the addition of cornflour and vinegar which gives this unusual texture.

*Armenian Pork;
Party Pavlova*

5 Meanwhile, prepare the topping. Whip the creams together until they just hold their shape. Put the peaches or nectarines, strawberries and kiwi fruit in a bowl with the grapes, add the liqueur, orange rind and juice with sugar to taste and fold in very gently to mix.

6 Just before serving, spread or pipe the cream in the centre of the pavlova, then top with the fruit.

A The meringue base can be made up to 4 days in advance and stored in an airtight tin; if you do not have a tin large enough, then you could bake the mixture in 2 × 18 cm (7 inch) tins and make 2 separate pavlovas.

PINA COLADA ICE CREAM

Serves 6

| 50 g (2 oz) creamed coconut |
| 3 tablespoons dark rum |
| 5 canned pineapple rings in natural juice, with 2 tablespoons juice reserved |
| 4 egg whites |
| 75 g (3 oz) caster sugar |
| 300 ml (½ pint) double cream |

Preparation time: *about 30 minutes, plus overnight freezing*
Cooking time: *2-3 minutes*

1 Cut the creamed coconut into small pieces and place in a saucepan with the rum. Heat gently, stirring, until the coconut melts. Cool.

2 Work the pineapple and juice to a purée in a blender or food processor. Add the coconut and rum mixture and work again to combine. Pour into a large bowl and set aside.

3 Put the egg whites in a separate large bowl and beat until very stiff and standing in peaks. Add the sugar and beat again until shiny.

4 Pour the cream into another bowl and whip until it just holds its shape. Fold into the pineapple mixture. Add the stiffly beaten egg whites and fold into the mixture until evenly combined. Transfer to a rigid container, cover and freeze overnight. **F** Serve straight from the freezer.

F The ice cream can be stored in the freezer for up to 1 month.

Everyone knows the famous American cocktail, pina colada. Made from rum, crushed pineapple, cream of coconut and cream, it is served in tall glasses with a straw, heavily decorated with pineapple pieces, cherries and cocktail parasols, etc. This ice cream contains the same ingredients as the cocktail, so it would be fun to decorate the serving glasses or dishes similarly.

61

CLASSIC COOK

These two classic recipes are perfect for lunchtime entertaining and both dishes can be made well in advance.

Poaching and glazing a whole salmon may seem a daunting prospect, but it is actually quite simple. All that is needed is time and patience with the poaching, skinning and boning, then a little care with the presentation. No particular skills are required, and the end result is really impressive. If you do not have a fish kettle for poaching the salmon, use a large roasting tin placed across two hobs, if necessary.

Duck liver pâté with orange is simplicity itself to make. Rich and buttery, it has a distinctive, tangy citrus flavour, which contrasts perfectly with the richness of duck livers. This type of pâté will become one of the all-time favourites.

Duck Liver Pâté with Orange and melba toast; Glazed Poached Salmon

DUCK LIVER PÂTÉ WITH ORANGE

Serves 8-10
350 g (12 oz) unsalted butter
1 large onion, peeled and roughly chopped
2-3 garlic cloves, peeled and roughly chopped
450 g (1 lb) duck or chicken livers
3 oranges
6 tablespoons brandy
2 teaspoons dried mixed herbs
salt
freshly ground black pepper

Preparation time: *about 20 minutes, plus cooling and chilling*
Cooking time: *about 25 minutes*

1 Melt the butter gently in a heavy-based saucepan. Pour three-quarters into a blender or food processor.
2 Add the onion and garlic to the pan and fry gently until soft. Add the livers and fry for about 10 minutes, stirring constantly, until just cooked.
3 Transfer the contents of the frying pan to the blender. Add the finely grated rind of 2 of the oranges, 3 tablespoons each orange juice and brandy, the herbs and salt and pepper to taste. Work to a smooth purée. Pour into a 1.2 litre (2 pint) terrine and leave until cold.
4 Slice the third orange into thin rings and squeeze the juice from the remainder. Put the orange slices and juice in a clean pan with the remaining brandy. Simmer gently until the orange

If you find duck livers difficult to obtain, you can use chicken livers just as well, in which case you could use lemon instead of the orange.

To make melba toast: toast medium slices of white or brown bread on both sides. Trim off and discard the crusts and cut carefully through the untoasted centres. Grill the untoasted surfaces until golden and the edges of the toast curl up.

is tender and the liquid reduced to a syrupy glaze.

5 Arrange the orange slices on top of the pâté and brush with the glaze. Cool, then chill in the refrigerator. **A** **F**

6 Serve with melba toast (see left). **A** The pâté can be made up to 3 days in advance. Store in the refrigerator. **F** Cover the terrine, then overwrap tightly. Freeze for up to 3 months. Thaw in the refrigerator overnight.

GLAZED POACHED SALMON

Serves 6

1 whole salmon, weighing 1.25 kg (3 lb), cleaned
1 × 25 g (1 oz) sachet aspic powder
½-¾ cucumber
1 canned red pimiento, well drained
1 stuffed olive
Court-bouillon:
600 ml (1 pint) water
300 ml (½ pint) dry white wine
2 slices of lemon
1 carrot, sliced
1 small onion, peeled and stuck with a clove
1 bouquet garni
6 black peppercorns
1 teaspoon salt

Preparation time: *about 1 hour, plus cooling*
Cooking time: *about 50 minutes*

1 Weigh the cleaned fish and calculate the poaching time, allowing 10 minutes per 450 g (1 lb).

2 First make the court-bouillon. Put all the ingredients in a saucepan and bring to the boil. Cover and simmer for 20 minutes. Leave until just warm.

3 Wrap the salmon loosely in muslin. Put the salmon in a fish kettle, or large roasting tin into which it fits comfortably without curling. Strain in the warm court-bouillon, and add warm water to cover the fish, if necessary. Cover with a lid or foil and simmer over gentle heat for the calculated poaching time. (Do not allow the liquid to boil or the salmon flesh will break up.) Allow the fish to cool in the court-bouillon.

4 Lift the salmon carefully on to a board covered with greaseproof paper and unwrap. Strain the court-bouillon and reserve. Skin and bone the salmon (see below). **A** Transfer the fish care-

fully to a serving platter.

5 Make up the aspic jelly according to packet instructions, using the reserved court-bouillon instead of water. Leave until just on the point of setting. Meanwhile, slice the cucumber very thinly, then cut each slice in half.

6 Brush the exposed flesh of the salmon with the liquid aspic jelly. Dip the cucumber slices one at a time in more aspic jelly, then place on the salmon. Secure in place with tooth picks if necessary, then brush more aspic jelly over the cucumber slices.

7 Cut the pimiento in strips and place over the gills of the salmon and across the tail. Remove the eye and replace with a slice of stuffed olive. Brush all over the head and collar of the salmon with aspic. Chill or keep very cold. **A**

8 Serve as a centrepiece for a lunch party with homemade mayonnaise (page 40), and potato and watercress salad. If you wish make up extra aspic jelly, chill it until set, then chop on dampened greaseproof paper. Serve around the salmon.

A The salmon will keep fresh in the refrigerator for up to 2 days, either before or after decorating. If keeping undecorated, cover loosely with foil.

When ordering a whole salmon allow 175-225 g (6-8 oz) per person (uncleaned weight). Salmon trout and young salmon (grilse) are more widely available than salmon – and less expensive. Both can be used in exactly the same way as salmon. Ask the fishmonger to clean the fish and remove the gills, leaving the head and tail on. When you get home, wash the fish well to remove any traces of blood inside. Vandyke the tail by cutting a 'V' shape out of the centre with kitchen scissors.

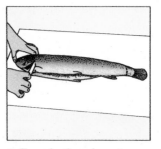

1 *Transfer the salmon to a sheet of greaseproof paper. Slit the salmon skin behind the gills and round the tail.*

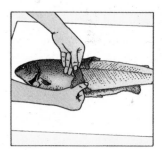

2 *Carefully peel off the skin from the top side. Leave the head and tail intact and take care not to damage the flesh.*

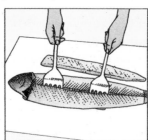

3 *Cut through the flesh along the backbone. Using fish slices, lift off the 2 fillets on either side of the backbone.*

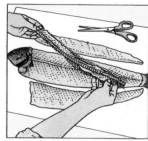

4 *Snip the backbone free at the head and tail end. Then carefully lift out and discard. Replace the fillets.*

INDEX

ACKNOWLEDGEMENTS

Photography: Simon de Courcy Wheeler
Photographic styling: Fiona Skrine
Preparation of food for photography: Poppy
and Jennie Shapter
Illustrations: Will Giles
The publishers would also like to thank the
following companies for the loan of props for
photography:
The Cocktail Shop, 30 Neal Street, London
WC2;
Elizabeth David, 46 Bourne Street, London
SW1;
The Glass House, 65 Long Acre, London WC2;
David Mellor, 4 Sloane Square, London SW1